THE GILGAMESH CYCLE

The fully restored Epic of Gilgamesh

a 5,000 year old epic poem
with zodiacal connections

TIMOTHY J. STEPHANY

ISBN-13: 978-1481893596
ISBN-10: 1481893599

Printed in the United States of America by Createspace

http://www.timothyjstephany.com

Contents

other books by TIMOTHY J. STEPHANY

Enuma Elish: The Babylonian Creation Epic

The Sources Bible: Genesis through Kings (ASV)

The Holy Bible Revealed I: Genesis through Kings with Sources

The Holy Bible Revealed II: Compositional History

The Yahweh Document: The Holy Bible's First Edition

The Levi Document: The Earliest Biblical Source

The Eden Enigma: A Dialogue

Roar of the Tempests: A Dialogue

The Death of King David: A Dialogue

The Zodiac Mysteries

Blood & Incest: The Unholy Beginning of the Universe

Introduction

The Gilgamesh Cycle, known typically as 'The Epic of Gilgamesh', is a work represented in writing over 4,000 years ago.* Prior to when it was first written down there is no way of determining precisely at what point it might have emerged in human history, although there are defensible reasons to believe it ties in with some of the earliest myths told by the human race. (The origin of the mythical characters Gilgamesh and Enkidu is discussed in the book *Blood & Incest: The Unholy Beginning of the Universe.*) Yet, even if we might claim that the Gilgamesh Cycle must have existed in some recognizable form 5,000 years ago, it is not untenable to suppose that some traces of its mythical vignettes extend back even another 5,000 years.

    The extraordinary preservation of the Cycle is the result of the relatively recent recovery of thousands of clay tablets from the former cities of ancient Mesopotamia. The earliest surviving version is the Sumerian which appears in the early 2nd millennium BC, and is followed by the Old Babylonian version which was likewise written down in the 2nd millennium. The most complete of the texts, the Akkadian, which emerged during the time of the Assyrian Empire, is rather from the 8th and 7th centuries BC, while other fragments come from even later periods. So the stories of Gilgamesh, in written form, are found extending over a span of 2,000 years; although knowledge of the epic appears to have slowly succumbed to the dissolutions of time, coming to light to the world again, and likewise to be readable again, only in the 19th century of our own era.

    Yet what precisely is the Gilgamesh Cycle as it was comprehended in the past compared to how it is understood today? Certainly it is a human story, despite its myriad of mythic settings; Gilgamesh in it rather takes on the role of Everyman, in a story which spans his life from youth to maturity, and builds into a quest for eternal youth, which is perhaps an objective as yet not entirely cast off by the pursuits of modern science. The story is thus timeless to humanity, as humanity is, and yet at the same time it remains difficult to otherwise bridge the conceptual differences between ancient Mesopotamia and the modern world, if not from the mere fact that we not only exist in an almost entirely dissimilar technological world, but also with different cultural conceptions, religions, science, and outlook; though perhaps not *entirely* different. But it is important to appreciate that the Mesopotamians were the 'inventors' of civilization and as such

---

* It is not obvious that the varied episodes of Gilgamesh were yet united in ancient Sumer. In the Sumerian king lists Gilgamesh is listed as one of the historical kings of Uruk, but there is no way to judge whether or not this refers to a legendary king.

experienced for the first time both the benefits and miseries, conventions and consequences of adopting to life in cities, and some of these enter into the context of the Cycle narrative itself. We find too the very notion of a walled city so unusual that its appearance caused them to liken it to a sheep pen, and thus it is referred to as Uruk, the Sheep Pen.

In addition, when considering its age, as we now deem it the first of epics, still we are most aware of the analogous literature which followed, and thus it is relevant to recognize that a foremost tale might well be consequential to those we know well, even when it might not be quite so refined in the manner we have become accustomed to. Yet the story does possess everything which might be required from a full-blown heroic epic, though it remains largely episodic and in some manner still inaccessible through its fragmentary preservation. Still, as it has not otherwise survived in Western Civilization, most have yet to become aware of the characters Gilgamesh or Enkidu. But it must be presumed that every heroic drama owes something to one that has such an early origin and was so widespread in the ancient world. Yet what perhaps strikes into our American sentiments most severely is not so much the cultural and conceptual differences as much as its pervading mainstay of pessimism. At least, despite its import, the epic itself is one which emerges lacking the glorious finale of triumph. This appears to be the most significant reason, perhaps, apart from its fragmentary condition, which has prevented it from gaining greater recognition and interest. Certainly, in our culture the most prevalent mythical stories still come out of the Biblical texts, from which names are at least recognized at once, if not the stories themselves rudimentarily summarized.

This edition attempts to remedy some of this, at least from the point of view of bringing together a version which endeavors to make the entire Gilgamesh Cycle complete, which is no simple task but certainly possible due to the well preserved Akkadian version. Although later than the prior versions, it is noticeably recorded upon 12 tablets, the first 11 of which form a continuous narrative, and the final of which was added later, being rendered largely from a Sumerian original. Still, even if one complete text of the Gilgamesh Cycle survived it would still not be *the* Gilgamesh Cycle because, as with any other myth, it is forever changing at different locations and in different times.

It is more curious to find the term 'authoritative' prefixing any text, especially within religious texts, which create a false sense that there exists one predominant version among variations. And what is utilized to establish the precedence of one text over others but that such a thing is 'agreed upon by scholars', or that it is the 'most numerous' among the texts which survive, or that it has been determined by some 'official' committee; or beyond these that it has come to be accepted through tradition or 'divine revelation'. Such considerations ought to teach us that the notion of assigning the term 'authoritative' to an arbitrary decision remains a hollow pursuit, perhaps as much as Gilgamesh's own quest for eternal youth, for any criterion used to argue that something ought to be accepted as the 'true' text is yet besieged by persistent disagreement. These arise not merely from the existence of different opinions or points of view, which might otherwise be overcome, but by the very nature of the decision, as it remains entirely subjective and unverifiable.

Thus while this version of the Gilgamesh Cycle is predominantly that of the Akkadian version, this is only because this version was the one that became relatively fixed in the ancient world for a thousand years, and thus too is the most complete text which has come down to us, so it will likely remain the 'standard version' of the epic. But it should not be viewed as quite the same as the *Iliad*, which we must accept was one among several epic tales concerning the Trojan War, but which is not only the one which survives but which has also been considered a superior work of literature, and as such it commands greater interest than a slew of other ancient works which fail to achieve or surmount the same literary heights. And so too while the Gilgamesh Cycle is itself deemed an epic due to its comparative length and heroic struggles, it need not be immediately comparable to either the *Iliad* or *Odyssey*.

As such there remains no persuasive reason to adhere to one single version, in an attempt to restore it alone, when worthy material is found within the others; and as such while following the Akkadian version predominantly, every attempt has been made to incorporate as much of the Old Babylonian version into it as well. This is certainly done to fill in gaps left by lacunae within the Akkadian tablets, but there is also inserted additional material not otherwise included within the Akkadian version, perhaps from dramatic considerations. There have, however, been only modest attempts made to smooth over the differences, so that there will arise minor inconsistencies due to discrepancies in the details between them. As such the Old Babylonian version's inclusion of Wer, Humbaba's guard, makes no appearance when they confront Humbaba but in references to him when the Old Babylonian version again emerges. (Though it is not even clear he was entirely absent from the Akkadian version due to lacunae within that text.) Likewise, there arises a discrepancy that Inanna (Akkadian Ishtar) in the Sumerian version refers to Gilgamesh as her brother, as likewise is Shamash. So the attempt here has not been to provide a retelling of any version of the epic but to provide as complete as possible a rendering of the original Gilgamesh Cycle, as far as things stand early in this millennium.

It should be pointed out that merely because the Sumerian amounts to the earliest rendering of the episodes of Gilgamesh in writing neither means that the composition does not precede that time, perhaps by centuries, nor that its episodic nature insists that they did not derive from a once unified collection. Consideration of this question causes us too to recognize that the sequence of episodes by no means appears to have arisen accidentally. Rather, each episode might be specifically referenced to the sequence of constellations found around the *ecliptic*, or 'cycle', which is the path of the sun. The requirement that the epic itself spanned 12 tablets implies an association with 12 zodiacal constellations, comprising those traversed by the sun within the year; even though this appears to have forced the addition of one further episode to assure that the requisite number of tablets was achieved. This was apparently accomplished through the copying of a further episode from off of Sumerian tablets which is in no way incorporated into the prior narrative, but is merely appended to it without a great deal of modification. It is perhaps due more to the importance of numerology; specifically the desire to make human achievements compatible with the divine order of the universe.

As to assessing which constellations have been included, it is important to be aware that most of the constellations which we are familiar with arise from the ancient ones of Greece and Rome, which were themselves borrowed from those known in the ancient Near East, including both Mesopotamia and Egypt. The Egyptian constellations are best known through an examination of the 'Dendera Zodiac' which presents pictorial representations of the constellations of the northern hemisphere, even though it dates from a much later period, only about 50 BC, and may have been influenced by the Greek ones. The constellations of Mesopotamia have been determined from a slew of clay tablets, just like the ones that record the Gilgamesh Cycle, which have been interpreted and published, as they were around 1000 BC, by Gavin White in his *Babylonian Star-Lore*, which provides some of the information for this book.

If you have not previously read 'The Epic of Gilgamesh' and would prefer to read it prior to learning something of its contents then skip ahead to the beginning of Tablet 1 and return to this point after you have finished reading the entire book, otherwise what follows associates the various episodes within the narrative to specific constellations to reveal how they correspond.

The specific constellations referenced can be more readily determined once the most obvious connections are identified; in other words, to associate anything which might be more easily linked with a specific constellation, then work out the other intervening ones. This could cause one to conclude that the Bull of Heaven must immediately be *Taurus*, which he clearly is; however it remains difficult to establish a meaningful sequence from this assignment for the remainder of the constellations. Yet if *Taurus* is instead associated with Gilgamesh in Tablet 1, specifically referred to as a wild bull, then we might more meaningfully traverse our way around the *ecliptic* from here. So we find that *Orion* corresponds to the hunter who first spies Enkidu in the wilderness, while *Auriga* (who carries three goats) represents the shepherds he meets on his crossover to civilization.[1] The following confrontation between Gilgamesh with Enkidu, with them subsequently becoming brothers, would then be *Gemini*. The lions which they confront at the mountain passes would most certainly be *Leo*. Then this is followed by their confrontation with the demon Humbaba which could be *Ursa Major* (see **Roar of the Tempests**). The reason for this assignment is that in other mythological traditions *Ursa Major* is still included as a constellation of the zodiac, aligned with and most often replacing *Cancer*, however, because of its position it can also follow rather than precede the lion (see **Roar of the Tempests** and **The Death of King David**). Yet *Cancer* too represented in ancient Mesopotamia the Tigris and Euphrates rivers, the latter which was followed by Gilgamesh and Enkidu on their journey to Humbaba.[2] Ishtar would then be *Virgo*, representing the goddess herself, with the barley stalk as a symbol of agriculture, where now *Taurus*, which lies directly opposite, becomes the Bull of Heaven.* However, we might also associate *Ursa Major* with the thigh of the Bull of Heaven, which is the constellation known in Ancient Egypt as 'The Thigh'. This could then mean that Humbaba was associated not with *Ursa Major* but with the "Sphinx", appearing as a cherubic creature lying midway between *Leo* and *Virgo* (see **Blood & Incest**). *Libra* would then correspond with the death of Enkidu, which might not make sense at first, given that they are scales; however this also has something to do with the underworld Abyss, which is discussed in **The Zodiac Mysteries**; while the Scorpion who holds the balance was connected with death, the descent into the underworld, and lamentation.[3] The next obvious connection can be made between *Scorpius* and the scorpion men encountered by Gilgamesh in Tablet 9. Then *Sagittarius* corresponds to the beer-maid Siduri, who is actually equivalent somewhat with Athena, or the constellation of the 'Huntress' (see **The Zodiac Mysteries**), and the tree of the Hesperides (see **The Eden Enigma**). This also fits with Ishtar as goddess of war, for Siduri was known as 'Ishtar of wisdom'. Then immediately adjacent to *Sagittarius* is *Corona Australis*, known in ancient Mesopotamia as the 'Cargo Boat', which would fit with the craft piloted by Urshanabi, and which transports Gilgamesh to the land of Utnapishtim, the faraway, the Mesopotamian Noah. Continuing on next is *Capricornus* which again appears to fail to match with the narrative requirements, yet this constellation also seems to represent a marsh and the Underworld (see **The Zodiac Mysteries**), and thus the Waters of Doom. This then leads us to Utnapishtim, as *Aquarius* represents his recollection of the story of the Great Flood, and this particular constellation is likewise associated with Deucalion and the Flood.[4] Then we arrive at the most interesting point of all: the two constellations *Pegasus* and *Pisces*; for it is the 'Great Square' of *Pegasus* which constitutes the 'Field of the Blessed' and 'source of the rivers' (see **The Eden Enigma**) and likewise the home of Utnapishtim. Yet this is also the region of the heavens associated with eternal life and certainly corresponds to the Fountain of Life from the *Arabian Nights'* "Tale of

---

* Around 2000 BC the 'axis' of the stars (pole star) would have been nearer to *Ursa Major*.

Buluqiya" (see *The Zodiac Mysteries*). But more so this is the location of the portal through which one might gain access to the Abyss (Apsu), which is spoken of concerning Gilgamesh, who goes down the 'pipe' ('*ratu*'), and which might be identified as the circlet of the 'western fish' of *Pisces* (see *The Eden Enigma* and *The Zodiac Mysteries*)[5] to fetch the plant of everlasting youth. This then leads to one final episode, which is the arrival of the snake that comes to steal the plant, occurring in the space between *Pisces* and *Taurus*; thus matching with *Cetus*, the sea dragon. (So this serpent itself may have lived within the channel which led down to the Apsu.) It is interesting that at this point the snake who steals the plant of life is likened to a lion, since the sea-monster Cetus is depicted with the head and forepaws of a lion. Then there is the saying contained in 'The Words of Ahiqar' which states: No lion exists within the sea, and thus the sea-snake is referred to as the lion ('*labbu*').[6] This serpent could also have something to do with the constellation *Draco*, for this constellation never sets, which was taken in the ancient world as an indication of everlastingness. At which point we arrive again at *Taurus*, and it would appear that this location of commencement and termination was no accident, as we find too at this point the presence of the *Pleiades*, which is a star cluster identified with the New Year. Numerous cultures utilized the *Pleiades* to mark the commencement of their year including the Maya, the Aztecs, the ancient Tahitians and Hawaiians, the Maori of New Zealand, and the Caffres of South Africa. And although in ancient Babylonia the New Year commenced with the *vernal equinox*, around 4000 BC this event corresponded with the rising of the *Pleiades*. The stars of the *Pleiades*, associated with the Moon, were also used to designate the starting point for the 28 mansions of the moon. And in the ancient Sumerian tale of Gilgamesh these stars are even given to him by the sun god Shamash to guide him on his passage to the east.[7] This recollects too how Gilgamesh makes a point of referencing the significance of the New Year's festival prior to commencing his journey to confront the guardian of the Pine Forest, Humbaba. Thus we can summarize these 12 connections in the following table:

constellation	depiction
Taurus	Gilgamesh
Gemini	Gilgamesh and Enkidu
Leo	Lions in mountain passes
Ursa Major or 'Sphinx'	Humbaba
Virgo	Ishtar and Bull of Heaven
Libra	Enkidu's death
Scorpius	Scorpion men
Sagittarius	Beer-maid Siduri
Capricornus	Waters of Doom
Aquarius	Great Flood
Pegasus/Pisces	Land of Utnapishtim
Cetus	Snake

So concerning the method by which the entire Gilgamesh Cycle was reconstructed, it has relied both upon the rendition within *Myths from Mesopotamia* by Stephanie Dalley and that of Andrew George in his *The Epic of Gilgamesh*. Most modern translations end up being very similar to one another when working from complete lines, and greater discrepancies in translation arise in fragmentary ones, where the context remains difficult to identify. For the present version every attempt has been made to render for accuracy, but only as far as modern translations could be judged accurate, while attempting to piece together sensible meaning where contexts remain absent. In addition, every line has been composed not only to capture the meaning of the original but also to keep them of similar length, which likewise ought to aid in its reading. As such in certain instances the line content has been superficially extended so as to fill the entire space, while others have been contracted for the same reason, but without loss of meaning. Also it may be that one line has become two or two lines have been reduced to one in order to preserve this consistency and render clarity. This continues through the entirety of the Cycle apart from Tablet 12 where some of the lines are rendered more briefly so as to prevent generally unappealing and inappropriate wordiness.

As for lines which have to be reconstructed there remain only three ways of dealing with these: the first is to borrow from alternate versions of the Cycle from different locations and centuries; the second is to reproduce duplicated sections from within the same text, which is possible given the compositional style; while third and least reliable is to add 'continuity insertions' to fill in the gaps so as to aid the reading and understanding of the epic. These 'insertions' might rely upon discontinuous fragments, sometimes upon narrative expectations, but some others upon mere context and, where possible, isolated words. As such, depending upon which has been utilized, some reconstructions will remain quite close, at least in broad content, to the original story; while others will differ dramatically in terms of wording, content, and implication; however, every attempt has been made to use the information available to make the best restoration of the text without the insertion of misplaced content intrusions. This, of course, relies upon a certain amount of imagination but likewise imitation of substance and style, supported too, as it is, by a considerable mythological consciousness.

Upon the pages the first of these is distinguished by how it has been notated in the sideline; the second are indicated by utilizing bold font, with the original source being given in the sideline in parentheses; the third is shown in bold when relying upon certain remaining fragments within the line, while those which constitute an entirely modern rendering appear with a dash (-) in the sideline. The sideline information is summarized in the following table:

/A	Akkadian version
/B	Old Babylonian version
/H	Hittite version
/S	Sumerian version
/L	'late' version (after Akkadian)
/(A)	Lines transposed from within the Akkadian text
/A, **B**	Partial line from Akkadian with Old Babylonian given in bold
/-	Lines from discontinuous fragments or modern renderings

As for how well this effort achieves completeness of the entire Gilgamesh Cycle, it is difficult to determine precisely, as none of the versions are of the same length and so too none of them is complete. However, from utilizing the Akkadian version as a basis, the number of columns is six per tablet, but the number of lines per column varies considerably. In addition, estimating lines per tablet are likewise imprecise if the final, or sixth, column is missing, because then there remains no way to estimate how many lines it might have contained, being as it is the terminating column. As such an estimate of length might be roughly determined by assuming that column length can be approximated by the mean; and that for column six that the number of lines, it could be considered, would be randomly distributed about the mean. Although this still does not make it an accurate calculation, from this it can be approximated at about 3,000 lines for the entire poem. The number of lines within this particular rendition including all original and reconstructed lines, however, can be precisely determined. Excluding the expansion of Tablet 12, this version is roughly 2,900 lines and as such falls slightly short of the Akkadian version. But including all lines is runs just over 3,000 lines, and thus represents the best attempt to restore the character of the Gilgamesh Cycle so as to allow modern audiences to read it and appraise it for what it is, or was, and, surely, will be.

THE GILGAMESH CYCLE

TABLET 1

Of him who gazed upon the Abyss, which underlies the world,	/A
Who came to know **all things**, and gained wisdom in everything,	/A
Of Gilgamesh who gazed upon the Deep underlying the world,	/A
Who came to know **all things**, and gained wisdom in everything,	/A
When he **set out and explored the** many lands **of the vast world**	/A
He who experienced everything and came to gain high wisdom,	/A
He found what had been kept secret, he uncovered the obscured	/A
And returned with stories even of the era before the Great Flood	/A
After travelling long distances, in the end he tired and refrained	/A
And chiseled all of his hard-won deeds upon a memorial stone	/A
He caused the walls of Uruk, called the Sheep Pen, to be built	/A
And too the walls of the holy house Eanna,* an unmatched jewel	/A
You can see its side there, which spans it like a copper stripe	/A
Evaluate its fortifications, for there are none others like them	/A
And there too is the stepping stone, which has stood forever	/A
Then make your way to Eanna, the sanctified shrine of Ishtar,	/A
For there will arise no man nor monarch who could surpass it	/A
Climb upon the great wall of Uruk and walk the entire circuit	/A
Take a look for yourself at the foundation stones and the bricks	/A
You will see for yourself that these are the best of bricks, baked!	/A
The Seven Sages being the only ones who could have set its base	/A
Within is one square mile of housing, one square mile of orchard,	/A

---

* The structure housing Ishtar's temple

3

Another square mile of clay pits, not to mention the courtyard /A

This being the square in the temple of Ishtar, Queen of Heaven /A

The temple grounds and the three square miles make up Uruk /A

Seek therein, for there you will find a copper box holding tablets /A

Release the bronze catch, and open the lid to bare the mysteries /A

Remove from there the tablet made of *lapis lazuli* and peruse it /A

It reveals the story of a man who endured, Gilgamesh by name /A

He was a far better king than any, a warlord of huge proportion /A

He was of mighty form born in Uruk, a raging wild bull of a man /A

When he marched he walked before his people to lead the way /A

And stood behind them, lending support and encouragement /A

Like the firm meshing of a net, he provided security to his men /A

Like the wild flood-waters, strong enough to topple stone walls, /A

He was the ideal strong man, Gilgamesh, son of Lugalbanda /A

Also being the child of the high and untamed wild cow Ninsun /A

Gilgamesh is the name of him who was second to none in deeds /A

Who made passes through mountains and into them dug pits /A

He made his way across the ocean until he reached the dawn /A

He set eyes upon the edge of the world, looking for eternal life /A

By his strength he went distances to find faraway Utnapishtim /A

He restored the flood-spoiled holy places to their former glory /A

Establishing for the people the holy rituals of the mystic order /A

Not one among the kings of the world could compare to him /A

Who can rightfully avow himself as high king but Gilgamesh! /A

For he was marked at birth to acquire for himself great fame /A

Tablet I

He being one-third a mortal while the rest of him was divine /A

Belet-ili,* it was who determined what form his body would take /A

His facial features were rendered flawless by wise Nudimmud† /A

His countenance was confident, **his looks firm and inflexible** /A

Given the radiance of Shamash, and the strong will of Adad, /-‡

So too were his feet immense, his legs lofty, and his stride wide /H

Towering in stature high above the heads of the common man /-

His face was bearded like **thatch**; his hair burgeoned **as barley** /H

Standing tall he made a fine display, exceptional for a mortal /H

And as his body was lofty so too the haughtiness he displayed /-

Within the walls of Uruk he would strut about with great show, /A

Setting himself as the top dog, his head reared like a buffalo's /A

None could claim to be his equal, and engaging in war games /A

When he took his weapon, his fellows would have to take theirs /A

And the young men of Uruk were beset even in their **home-lives** /A

For Gilgamesh would not allow any young man to aid his father /A

Rather, all through the day and night he lorded over the people /A

He being, as he was, the shepherd of wide Uruk, the Sheep Pen, /A

He being, as he was, their shepherd, yet **still he was overbearing** /A

Gilgamesh would not allow **any young girl to help her** mother /A

Their cry raised high so that even the gods were the recipients /A

---

* The mother goddess, also called Aruru below, and equivalent to Mami

† Another name for Ea, or Enki, god of water

‡ These missing lines incorporate details from a Hittite version; Shamash is the sun and Adad the storm god.

Above all the mightiest; more agile, clever, and indefatigable /A

Gilgamesh could also not keep away from the braided heads /A

Neither to spare the warrior's lasses, nor leave brides undefiled /A

Their cry raised high so that even the gods were the recipients /A

The gods in heaven **heard all concerning** Uruk's prideful king /A

"Is it **Aruru** who takes responsibility for this menacing bull? /A

Could there be one who is his equal; engaging in his war games /A

When he takes his weapon, his fellows must also take theirs /A

Gilgamesh will not permit any young man to go aid his father /A

He being, as he is, the shepherd of wide Uruk, the Sheep Pen, /A

He being, as he is, their shepherd, and yet **still he is overbearing** /A

Above all the mightiest; more agile, clever, and indefatigable /A

And Gilgamesh also cannot keep away from the braided heads /A

Neither to spare the warrior's lasses, nor leave brides undefiled." /A

Such does almighty Anu hear when he listens to their grievances /A[*]

Then the cry went to the grand Aruru, "Aruru, you made **man**, /A

So produce a rival who can defy him, equal in temper and tone /A

That they may come to duel one another, and leave Uruk alone!" /A

Aruru listened to their pleas and she envisaged Anu's words /A

After cleaning both of her hands, Aruru drew off a piece of clay /A

And threw it forth so that it flew to the secluded countryside /A

---

[*] The following comes from an alternate version of the text, but amounts to repetition of what follows:

> (Anu spoke,) "**Let** us send for the grand **Aruru, for she made** man,
>
> **To produce a rival** who is exceedingly strong, **equal to Gilgamesh,**
>
> **So that** he might duel **against him,** and Uruk will no longer suffer!"

Tablet I

Thus she made a man who was primal, the combatant Enkidu   /A

He who was produced by a whisper, the lightning of Nimrod   /A

The entirety of his body was covered by a coarse shaggy coat,   /A

And from his head fell locks of hair the length of any woman's   /A

They were tresses which were abundant as the growing wheat   /A

With no knowledge of men nor of nation, dressed only in skins   /A

He ate with gazelles and drank at the watering hole with cattle   /A

Along with the other beasts he eagerly bent to drink at the pool   /A

There a hunter and trapper saw him up close at the water's edge   /A

And again recognized this very same man three days in a row   /A

When this huntsman was perplexed, to see him with the herds,   /A

He left in bewilderment, making his way back to his dwelling   /A

But this made him uneasy, he kept to himself and spoke not   /A

There was a sign of anguish in his face, uneasiness in his gaze   /A

He harbored a kind of misery which imbued his deepest frame   /A

The expression he took was like that of a world-worn traveler   /A

This hunter spoke with his father so his voice might be heard,   /A

"Father, I saw a young man who came **down from the uplands**,   /A

When he strove on land he showed both strength and vitality   /A

And he had an almighty power in him like the lightning of Anu   /A

There I see him always wandering upon the mountainous range   /A

Whenever I see him he's munching plants along with the beasts   /A

When I see him he splashes in the water with the rest of them   /A

But I remain far too fearful of him to attempt approaching him   /A

7

Yet he is the one who keeps filling the pits I excavate to entrap /A

He is also the same one who removes all of the snares that I set /A

By doing so he aids the grazers, and other untamed creatures /A

So that they are able to evade all my attempts to capture them /A

That I might accomplish naught in those uncultivated places." /A

The father of the hunter listened, and gave him a ready reply, /A

"Go to the King of Uruk, Gilgamesh, for that land is his territory /A

His strength is also an almighty power, like Anu's lightning /A

So go now and set forth on your way to the kingdom of Uruk /A

For there you will find such women who sap the vitality of men /A

There you will find Shamhat the prostitute, take her with you, /A

You must remain hidden until the coming of this burly man, /A

Until he makes his way to the watering hole with the buffalo /A

She must take off her clothing before him, make herself naked /A

So when he sets his eyes upon her he will move in closer to her /A

Then wild beasts, his former kin, will be as strangers to him." /A

The youth listened to every word of advice his father gave him /A

Then the hunter set forth to seek his regal majesty, Gilgamesh /A

He made his way on the road, to the city of Uruk, the Sheep Pen /A

There he came into the court of Gilgamesh, conveying to him, /A

"I saw a young man who descended down from the uplands, /A

When he strove on land he showed both strength and vitality /A

And he had an almighty power in him like the lightning of Anu /A

But I remain far too fearful of him to attempt approaching him /A

Yet he is the one who keeps filling the pits I excavate to entrap /A

Tablet I

He is also the one who removes all of the snares that I have set /A

By doing so he aids the grazers, and other untamed creatures /A

So that they are able to evade all my attempts to capture them /A

That I might accomplish naught in those uncultivated places." /A

So after listening Gilgamesh spoke to this man, to the hunter, /A

"Proceed huntsman, and take with you Shamhat the prostitute, /A

So that when he makes his way to the watering hole with buffalo, /A

She must remove her clothing before him, making herself naked /A

And when he sets his eyes upon her he will move in closer to her /A

Then wild beasts, his former kin, will be as strangers to him." /A

So the hunter proceeded, taking with him Shamhat the harlot /A

Together they walked the road and traversed the entire span /A

So that in three day's time they had arrived at their destination /A

The hunter and the harlot concealed themselves and waited /A

They were there for a day, then two, sitting near the water hole /A

Until buffalo came down to the pool's edge and began to drink /A

Likewise, wild animals came to the water to alleviate their thirst /A

So too the one who lived in the uplands, the wild man Enkidu, /A

Him who ate with gazelles and drank at the water with cattle /A

With the other beasts he bent low to drink for his sustenance /A

And Shamhat first set her eyes upon this primeval cave man /A

A savage young man from the vast stretches of the wilderness, /A

"That's him, Shamhat, so now is the time to bare your breasts /A

Angling your thighs enough that he might see you splendidly /A

9

But refrain from retreating before him, show interest instead,   /A

For when he sees you he will approach you from sheer instinct   /A

Then shed your clothing entirely, allow him to mount your hill   /A

And treat this wild man in just the way women favorably do   /A

That the wild beasts, his former kin, will be as strangers to him   /A

He won't refrain from unleashing his lustful desires upon you."   /A

She undid her garment, angling her thighs; he spied her naked   /A

And she did not retreat before him, but rather showed interest   /A

Then shed her clothing entirely, allowing him to mount her hill   /A

She treated this wild man in just the way women favorably do   /A

He didn't refrain from unleashing his lustful desires upon her   /A

For six days and intervening nights was he enflamed with lust   /A

Repeatedly forcing his vigorous ejaculations within Shamhat   /A

By which time he had been thoroughly fulfilled of her allure   /A

Then he made his way to return to the wild ways of the beasts   /A

But when the gazelles saw Enkidu approach, they scampered   /A

And no longer did the buffalo of the wilderness approach him   /A

Now his body was no longer hirsute, his skin now far too bright,   /A

While his legs, by which he ran with buffalo before, were slowed   /A

Enkidu could sense he had lost his vitality, unable to run apace   /A

Still he found his thoughts more profound, his mind more wise   /A

Realizing this he returned, sitting near to where the harlot stood   /A

The prostitute noticed the expression which lay upon his face   /A

And when she spoke to him he listened closely to what she said,   /A

"Now you have grown wise Enkidu, and are similar to the gods   /A

Tablet I

So why would you now still wander the wilderness with beasts? /A
Rather instead, I'll take you to the city of Uruk, the Sheep Pen /A
There you will be in civilization, where Anu and Ishtar reside /A
There you will find King Gilgamesh, a man foremost in strength /A
Who is himself like a buffalo, of supreme power among men." /A
Thus she spoke to him, and he found her words were agreeable /A
Knowing how he had changed, he now thought to make friends /A
So Enkidu raised his own voice, and spoke to the prostitute, /A
"Then let us go together, Shamhat, take me wherever you go /A
Let us go to civilization, where the gods Anu and Ishtar reside /A
Let us go to find King Gilgamesh, a man foremost in strength /A
Who is himself like a buffalo, of supreme power among men /A
And there I will confront him, **so let it be a contest of strength** /A
So thereby making it plain in Uruk that I be proven supreme /A
There I will go, and thereby I will change the course of destiny /A
And it will be that the one born in the wilderness **will prevail!**" /A
Then Shamhat said to him in reply, "Then come, let us travel, /A
Let me show you happiness and of all other diversions I know /A
Then let us travel, Enkidu, to the city of Uruk, the Sheep Pen /A
Where you will find the young men wearing splendid sashes /A
Where each day is a festival, and drums resound throughout /A
There the young women will display their fine bodies to entice /A
Bursting with elevated spirits of mirth, all are imbued with joy /A
Where at night the men of valor **sleep in peace and serenity** /A
You, dearest Enkidu, **have never known of** such a life as this /A

11

Let me lead you to Gilgamesh, the one of gladness and sadness   /A

Then you might see him yourself, and look upon his own face   /A

He is to me of such a handsome appearance, and distinguished   /A

So too I consider that his entire body is imbued with seduction   /A

But I say to you that he is much stronger of arm than you are   /A

You will not find him to be sleeping either by day or by night   /A

So, my dear Enkidu, change your mind from challenging him   /A

Gilgamesh is one favored by the sun god Shamash himself,   /A

On top of this Anu, Ellil, and Ea bestowed him with wisdom[*]   /A

"Even before you descended from the high mountainous tracts   /A

Gilgamesh had already had a dream concerning you in Uruk   /A

After he awoke he provided all the details of it to his mother,   /A

'O Mother, there was a dream which I witnessed last night   /A

There was an array of heavenly stars gathered around me   /A

And what was like the lightning from Anu falling above me   /A

But when I attempted to lift it up, it proved to be too weighty   /A

So I attempted to shift it, but even then it would not budge   /A

Around it I could see standing there all the citizens of Uruk,   /A

The population amassed over it, the men, and the youth too,   /A

And all of them were kissing its feet as though it were a baby   /A

But this thing too did I possess a dear affection for, like a wife,   /A

Then I took it up and brought it to you, setting it at your feet   /A

---

[*] Anu is the supreme god of the firmament and rules in heaven, Ellil is god of air and fire and rules upon earth, and Ea is god of water and rules in the Abyss (Apsu). Anu is the father of the storm god Adad.

Tablet I

Thereupon you deemed it to be my equal, by how you favored it.' /A

So the wise mother of Gilgamesh, who knew all, now spoke, /A

The untamed heifer Ninsun, who knew all, said to Gilgamesh, /A

'My son, when you saw an array of stars gathered around you /A

And what was like the lightning from Anu falling above you /A

When you attempted to lift it up, it proved to be too weighty /A

When you attempted to shift it, even then it did not budge /A

Then you took it up and brought it to me, setting it at my feet /A

Thereupon I deemed it to be your equal, by how I favored it /A

But this thing did you have a dear affection for, like a wife /A

All this means is that a mighty companion will seek you out /A

One who holds the ability to preserve the lives of his friends /A

And who will prove supreme in the use of his arms anywhere /A

That his might could be compared to the lightning of Anu /A

And truly you will have a dear affection for him, like a wife, /A

But he will also be a companion who acts as your savior.' /A

When he had had a second dream he went to the goddess, /A

Then Gilgamesh raised his voice to be heard, to his mother, /A

'But Mother, I also had a second dream during the night /A

In this one a copper axe fell down into the streets of Uruk /A

It landed in the middle of the city and the folks gathered /A

The people of the entire land stood over it, amassed above it /A

Then I took it up and brought it to you, setting it at your feet /A

But this thing too did I possess a dear affection for, like a wife, /A

Thereupon you deemed it to be my equal, by how you favored it.' /A

So the wise mother of Gilgamesh, who knew all, now spoke, /A

The untamed heifer Ninsun, who knew all, said to Gilgamesh, /A

'The copper axe you saw in actuality represents a fellow man /A

And truly you will have a dear affection for him, like a wife, /A

And I will deem him to be your equal, by how I favor him /A

One who holds the ability to preserve the lives of his friends /A

And who will prove supreme in the use of his arms anywhere /A

That his might could be compared to the lightning of Anu.' /A

Then Gilgamesh raised his voice, speaking to his mother, /A

'Then so be it, by the word of Ellil, the supreme authority /A

By this will I come to have a friend to give me good counsel.' /A

And as such Ninsun recounted each of these dreams to me." /A

So Shamhat knew Gilgamesh's dreams and told it to Enkidu, /A

"The significance of these dreams is that you'll be dear friends." /A

(Shamhat took Enkidu to where he could gaze down upon Uruk)

TABLET II

Shamhat took Enkidu to where he could gaze down upon Uruk	/-[8]
Then she spoke so that her voice might be heard, to Enkidu,	/-
"Gilgamesh caused the walls of Uruk, the Sheep Pen, to be built	/(A)
And too the walls of the holy house Eanna, an unmatched jewel	/(A)
You can see its side there, which spans it like a copper stripe	/(A)
Evaluate its fortifications, for there are none others like them	/(A)
And there too is the stepping stone, which has stood forever	/(A)
Then make your way to Eanna, the sanctified shrine of Ishtar,	/(A)
For there will arise no man nor monarch who could surpass it	/(A)
Climb upon the great wall of Uruk and walk the entire circuit	/(A)
Take a look for yourself at the foundation stones and the bricks	/(A)
You will see for yourself that these are the best of bricks, baked!	/(A)
The Seven Sages being the only ones who could have set its base	/(A)
Within is one square mile of housing, one square mile of orchard,	/(A)
Another square mile of clay pits, not to mention the courtyard	/(A)
This being the square in the temple of Ishtar, Queen of Heaven	/(A)
The temple grounds and the three square miles make up Uruk."	/(A)
Enkidu thought in his heart that this place was not suitable	/-
Not knowing how he could live here rather than in the uplands	/-
Shamhat told him that he ought to ask such a thing of Ninlil	/-
Now Enkidu was in Tirannu,* he was kneeling and facing her	/A
As he looked up at the goddess he was overwhelmed with tears	/A

---

* A name for the kingdom of Uruk

He felt an odd divine power and thus he put his trust in Mulliltu[*]   /A

Enkidu spoke his words so that they might be heard by her alone   /-

How he had been born and grew up in the mountainous tracts   /-

How he had lived his life with the beasts and ran with the buffalo   /-

And why he must then leave this life he knew to now live in cities   /A

They jointly discussed the matter, and spoke together for a time   /A

And after coming to a decision he rose and then turned away   /A

Now knowing deep within his heart that he could not go back   /A

After this Shamhat then removed the two robes that draped her   /A, B[9]

One piece of clothing she gave to Enkidu that he might dress   /A, B

And the second piece of clothing Shamhat took to dress herself   /A, B

Then took him by the hand and, like a goddess, led him away   /A, B

To the dwelling of the shepherds, with a sheep's pen at hand   /A

And there the shepherds were all gathered round about him   /A

Who came from their own interest, saying among themselves,   /A

"How this burly young man is so much like Gilgamesh of form."   /A

"And so too of sturdy stature, with the fortitude of fortifications."   /A

"Surely he is one of those born in the mountainous uplands."   /A

"The strength of his arms is as great as the lightning of Anu."   /A

So then they placed food before him, but he did not reach for it   /A, B

So then they placed drink before him, but he did not touch it   /A, B

Enkidu showed no interest in it, but rather looked inquisitively   /A

He had never known anything of drinking beer nor eating bread   /B

This is something which he had never been taught when a boy   /B

---

[*] The goddess Ninlil, goddess of the atmosphere and wife of Ellil

Tablet II

He had rather known only the eating of raw meat for his hunger   /B

He had rather known only to drink the milk of cows for his thirst   /B

So the harlot then spoke that she might be heard, to Enkidu,   /B

"This is food you must eat, Enkidu, for it means your existence   /B

Likewise you must consume the beer, for it is the land's fortune."   /A

So then Enkidu took up the bread and ate it until he was full   /B

And took to drinking beer, until he had finished seven whole jars   /B

Then he fell back and was quite content, his heart was cheered,   /B

So now his face took on the look of a man who was rejuvenated,   /B

Covered his hairy body **with unguent**, anointed himself with oil,   /B

So from then on he became just like other men, dressing himself   /B

He took up the use of the war weapon and became like a hero   /B

Now allied with the society of men, he contended with the lions   /B

So the shepherds could sleep without worry during the nights   /B

With his arms he took on wolves **and frightened off predators**   /A, B

So that when the old herdsmen **lay to sleep, Enkidu kept watch**   /A, B

And he **was approached by a young** herder, **who spoke to him,**   /A, B

"You would rest content if you stayed here at home **amongst us**   /A

There's much going on in Uruk, the Sheep Pen, **you do not know."**   /A

Enkidu heard from him about the manner of Gilgamesh the king   /-[10]

He learned of both his splendor and arrogance, and his pastimes   /-

Shamhat told him that she knew something of the bed of Ishhara[*]   /-

But that they must learn more from someone who was let within   /-

---

[*] Goddess of marriage; another name for Ishtar

One who was allowed to enter the homes of the fathers-in-law	/-
So with her Enkidu went and waited, on the night she suggested	/-
Then while they were waiting she saw the young man appear	/-
Enkidu was glad and looked with his eyes and perceived him	/B
So he spoke to the prostitute, and made his voice heard, saying,	/B
"Shamhat, call the man over here, I would like to speak with him	/B
So I might find out what he might be doing and why he is here."	/B
She said she would call him by his name and shouted to him	/B
Then Enkidu went to where he was standing and spoke to him,	/B
"Young man, I merely wished to ask you where you were going	/B
And why you are expending yourself and in such a great hurry?"	/B
The young man replied to Enkidu, so his voice might be heard,	/B
"I do so because I've been invited to the father-in-law's house	/B
It is the fate of the people, where daughters-in-law are selected	/B
There I have the duty of keeping the ceremonial table supplied	/B
With all kinds of dishes and delicacies of the father-in-law's city	/B
And also for the king of wide and broad Uruk, the Sheep Pen	/B
So too I say, 'Open the way among the people for bridegrooms!	/B
Do this for the king of spacious Uruk, Gilgamesh is his name	/B
Open the way among the people for grooms, Gilgamesh comes!'	/B
And he will be the first to impregnate the future wife, the bride	/B
He shall be first to have her, the husband will only be second	/B
This arose from the decree which came from the word of Anu	/B
This was his birthright, his destiny, from the origin of his navel."[*]	/B

---

[*] That is, from the time his umbilical cord was cut

Tablet II

Upon hearing this from the young man, Enkidu's face went red	/B
He was now resolute to make his way through the gate of the city	/-[11]
Making himself ready for a confrontation with the bull of Uruk	/-
Asking the harlot to go with him, who knew the place very well	/-
As they went Enkidu took the lead and Shamhat followed him	/B
So he entered the wide and broad city of Uruk, the Sheep Pen	/B
When he walked through, all the population stood on every side	/B
As he was standing there in the street of Uruk they talked of him	/B
"Is he not just the same shape as Gilgamesh, if even a bit shorter	/B
But he also has bones which are thick, being from the mountains	/B
He has thus known only the eating of **raw meat for his hunger**	/B
He has thus known only to drink the milk of cows for his thirst	/B
Know that in Uruk, the Sheep Pen, there is no end to sacrifices	/B
Know that here in the city the young men are clean and purified	/B
Hear the *lusanum*-instrument play for the man who is honest!	/B
At last one has appeared who can challenge divine Gilgamesh!"	/B
So there he remained within the street of Uruk, **by the entrance**	/A
He waited at the threshold until the arrival of the mighty **bull**	/A
To block the entry **so that Gilgamesh would be unable to go by**	/A, B
And the entire citizenry of Uruk was there gathered about him	/A
The population amassed around him, the men and youth too,	/A
And all of them were kissing his feet as though he were a baby,	/A
When that young man **made his appearance at the threshold**	/A
Then was the bed made ready for an evening to honor Ishhara	/A
The king came there every night to engage with the young girls	/B

19

Yet there remained a man of equal strength for divine Gilgamesh   /A

Enkidu stood in front of the door of the father-in-law's dwelling   /A

Set on making sure that Gilgamesh had no way to get through   /A

So there by the door of the father-in-law's home they wrestled   /A

They came to grips within the street, there in the central square   /A

The fracas caused every wall and door-frame to shift and shake   /A[12]

Confronting one another like two bulls, hunkered and brawled   /B

Until Gilgamesh was forced down, his knee set upon the dirt   /B

Then his fury shriveled, he backed away, and then he withdrew,   /B

Enkidu spoke so that his voice might be heard, to Gilgamesh,   /B

"When your mother gave you birth, you were to be matchless   /B

The untamed heifer Ninsun, of the cow shed, assured you alone   /B

Would rise in supremacy, praised above all the fighting men   /B

The god Ellil declared that you would be the people's sovereign   /B

And who was meant to be a king among kings, outshining all   /B

But now a rival has arisen who has come up to challenge him   /-

So no longer might he boast of rising above and defeating any."   /-

And as Enkidu spoke a new realization arose within the king   /-

The pride of Gilgamesh now reduced to rubble, his eyes flooded   /-

When he finished speaking, they now kissed and were friends   /B[13]

Those gathered there grew emotional and overcome with tears   /B

Then the mother of Gilgamesh arrived, and he himself spoke,   /B

"This burly young man who descended down from the uplands,   /(A)

He strove on the land and showed both his strength and vitality   /(A)

Who has proven himself supreme in use of his arms anywhere /A

So that his might could be compared to the lightning of Anu /A

And so too his sturdy stature, with the fortitude of fortifications." /A

So the wise mother of Gilgamesh, who knew all, spoke to her son, /A

The untamed heifer Ninsun, who knew all, said to Gilgamesh, /A

"My son, within your gates **you have been honored as the king** /A

But you must accept that your fate is just the same as any man /A

You might cry in grief **now, but he will save the life of a friend** /A

He knows how to fight and can provide you good battle advice /(A)

While you hold **the staff of rule, with your servants and subjects,** /A

You are prideful within your gates, **having forsaken all humility."** /A

Overcome with heartfelt tears of woe, **deeply troubled he spoke,** /A

"Enkidu had no **other home but the wilderness in the uplands** /A

And from his head fell locks of hair the length of any woman's /A

This man born out in the wilderness, how could any beat him?" /A

And Enkidu was standing there, listening to every word he said /A

He pondered to himself, seated himself, and also began to weep /A

As his eyes too became greatly bleary from the rivulets of tears, /A

The muscles of his arms no longer rigid, his strength **abating,** /A

They then fell into embracing, and shook hands with each other /A

Then Gilgamesh spoke that his voice might be heard, to Enkidu, /B

"Please tell me why your eyes overflow **with such tears of woe** /A, B[14]

You too appear to be upset and are suffering a harsh anguish?" /B

Enkidu spoke so that his voice might be heard, to Gilgamesh, /B

"It is due to the wailing from your own grievance, my brother, /B

What has caused my neck to strain, my arms to become weak, /B

It is because of what I see that my strength has abandoned me." /B

Gilgamesh spoke so that his voice might be heard, to Enkidu, /B

"My friend, we are not meant to be adversaries of each other /-

Rather now that you have come to be in Uruk, the walled city, /-

You who have traversed the mountains, gone upon far ridges, /-

Walked with buffalo, must know the entrance to the Pine Forest /-

The killing of Humbaba **is something which I must endeavor** /B

It is this one, the guardian of the woods, whom I will challenge /B

And **this terror among the trees** who is the one I will mangle! /B

To achieve this I will strike down the mightiest of spruce trees /B

To make my way through the deep forest, **and discover his lair** /B

Then there will I challenge him, then there will we join in battle /-

With your guidance I'm sure I can find him and conquer him." /-

Enkidu spoke that his voice might be heard, saying to Gilgamesh, /B

"My dear friend, you must not make your way to the Pine Forest /B

When I went upon the mountain, when I walked with buffalo, /B

Its blackest depths terrified me; that dreaded wood extends far, /B

The journey much too dangerous for a mortal man, he would die /A

The one who guards the Pine Forest, Ellil made terrible to man /A

His voice roars like the storm-surge, his speech is a baleful fire, /A

His breath is death to man, he can hear as far as sixty leagues,[*] /A

Through the depths of the wood, who could trespass his forest? /A

---

[*] Following Dalley, a league here replacing a 'double-hour' (see Dalley 2000: 127)

22

For surely Humbaba is second in power only to Adad himself /A

Who even among the gods would be able to stand against him? /A

The one who guards the Pine Forest, Ellil made terrible to man /A

Anyone who found his way through would surely meet his end!" /A

Gilgamesh then raised his voice in reply, speaking to Enkidu, /A

"Then do you mean to say that **you would not show me the way?** /A[15]

Rather, help me make my way up the mountain, to walk ridges /-

Aid me in achieving my goal, to gain passage into the deep forest /-

I daresay that I could manage to tolerate its blackest depths /-

I would have no trouble fending off any beasts which beset us /-

To reach the lair of Humbaba, **that is as much as I am asking** /B

With an axe **we would be able to penetrate far into the woods** /B

You **can act as my guide, showing the right path we must take** /B

While I will **strike down the mightiest spruces to clear the way.**" /B

Then Enkidu spoke that he might be heard, saying to Gilgamesh, /B

"But there is no way we might come through the Pine Forest /B

There is a sentinel there by the name of Wer, **a veritable devil** /B

Not only is he of great strength, but he needs not a wink of sleep /B

Humbaba **need have no fear of anyone getting past** his guard /B

The great god Adad **is foremost, but surely Humbaba is second** /B

So there he **remains doing what the gods placed him there to do:** /B

To defend the Pine Forest, **and wield the** seven terror-weapons." /B

Then Gilgamesh spoke that he might be heard, saying to Enkidu, /B

"Who could hope to live as they do in heaven, my good friend? /B

It is only gods who are destined to live eternally with Shamash /B

We might count our days, and what man strives for is but empty /B

So do you find yourself fearful of death because of these things? /B

Has the mettle and gallantry of the hero inside abandoned you? /B

I then shall lead, while you cry out 'Go on farther and fear not.' /B

For I know that even if I were to die, I would yet be remembered /B

They would say, 'Gilgamesh engaged with and battled Humbaba!' /B

They will say, 'What nobility!', while you're from the wild lands /B

And when you had to face a lion, you knew precisely what to do /B

Even grown men have fled from you; so you're mettle is proven." /A

Enkidu raised his voice to be heard, and spoke to Gilgamesh, /-

"What then is the good of fame if you are not around to see it? /-

If we fled we would be cowards; even victory might be hollow." /-

Gilgamesh raised his voice to be heard and spoke to Enkidu, /A

"My friend, would there not be **women who called us saviors** /A

And would there not be children **who thought we were gods?"** /A

Enkidu raised his voice to be heard and **spoke to Gilgamesh,** /A

"My brother, were we to go **I fear one of us would lose his life** /A

Humbaba **is no mere beast, but is the worst sort of fire-demon."** /A

Gilgamesh raised his voice to be heard **and spoke to Enkidu,** /A

"My brother, we really should **not duel with words, let us see,** /A

It is right that we who are so formidable ought to welcome this /-

Who would rather be left to think that he were like a sour brat /-

For you said this before, and when you did it made me angry /B

So I will be the one who works hard, to lay low soaring spruces /B

And give rise to a deed which will live forever; so come with me, /B

Tablet II

I'll take you to the smiths, and there they'll forge arms for us." /B

So they took hands and went off together to arrive at the smiths /B

There the forgers considered together, putting together a plan, /A

They began with the casting of an iron-axe **of a formidable size** /A

Then twin-blade axes, using an entire *talent* of **bronze for each** /A

The swords made for them were a *talent* each, with **thick** belts /A

Each had well made rivets to bind them together, of thirty *minas* /B

Each had a golden **sheath** for his sword, which were thirty *minas* /B

Gilgamesh and Enkidu bore away a total of ten *talents* apiece /B

Then the seven gates of Uruk were closed and the bars bolted /B

Gilgamesh called the people together, the city's men assembled /B

They came together with great cheer in the wide streets of Uruk /B

Gilgamesh **foremost among them in** exhibiting blissful festivity /B

Gilgamesh spoke to the young men of Uruk, the elders listened, /A

"Hear me, you young men of Uruk, **who know the lure of fame** /A

I remain firm in my purpose, on the road to Humbaba will I go /A

I am willing to face an unknown danger, to ride a forsaken path /A

As I **have settled upon** my course, rather give me your blessings /A

That I might yet **see** your faces again **when all perils are past** /A

When I return **in glorious triumph** through the gates of Uruk /A

That at **some future time** I might **again see** the New Year's fair /A

And I might join with you in the celebration of the New Year /A

Let the festival procession commence, may **it spread** joy **to all** /A

Let loud cries of 'Halleluiah' resound **before the son of Ninsun**." /A

25

Then Enkidu advised the elders and heroic young men of Uruk,   /A

"Tell Gilgamesh that he must not make his way to the Pine Forest   /A

The journey is far too dangerous for a mortal man, he would die   /A

The one who guards the Pine Forest, Ellil made terrible to man   /A

His voice roars like the storm-surge, his speech is a baleful fire,   /A

His breath is death to man, he can hear as far as sixty leagues,   /A

Through the depths of the wood, who could trespass his forest?   /A

For surely Humbaba is second in power only to Adad himself   /A

Who even among the gods would be able to stand against him?   /A

The one who guards the Pine Forest, Ellil made terrible to man   /A

Anyone who found his way through would surely meet his end!"   /A

After listening, the wise men of Uruk rose to advise Gilgamesh,   /A

"Gilgamesh, you are **still young** and although you are now eager,   /A

You have no idea what adversities you will find **upon your quest**   /A

Humbaba's voice roars like the storm-surge, his speech is fire,   /A

His breath is death to man, he can hear as far as sixty leagues,   /A

Through the depths of the wood, who could trespass his forest?   /A

For surely Humbaba is second in power only to Adad himself,   /A

Who even among the gods would be able to stand against him?   /A

Ellil has made his sentinel Humbaba to be a terror to mankind   /A

Anyone who found his way through would surely meet his end!"   /A

Gilgamesh listened to every word the wise men of Uruk spoke,   /A

Then he looked over at his friend, making a wide smile at him   /B

"So do you think that this is how I should be making speeches   /B

Is it right that I too ought to be so fearful that I step backward?"   /B

Then Gilgamesh spoke to the wise men of Uruk, to the elders,   /(A)

"Hear me, you wise men of Uruk, who know the way of things,   /(A)

I remain firm in my purpose, on the road to Humbaba will I go   /(A)

I am willing to face an unknown danger, to ride a forsaken path   /(A)

As I have settled upon my course, rather give me your blessings   /(A)

That I might return, once again riding through the gates of Uruk."   /(A)

(Steadfast in his resolve the elders now determined to advise him)

TABLET III

Steadfast in his resolve the elders now determined to advise him, /-

"Heed us that you might come back to the safe haven of Uruk! /A

Gilgamesh, be not so bold to trust only in your physical might /A

After giving your eyes time to judge, trust in your first stroke /A

He who leads on the path will be the one who saves his friend /A

The one well familiar with the ways will be his brother's savior /A

Thus allow Enkidu to lead the way, he's familiar with the routes /A

He knows how to fight and can provide you good battle advice /A

So let Enkidu be a guardian to his friend and preserve your life /A

That you might come back safely, to return and satisfy brides, /A

So that we who advise might rely upon you to remain our king, /A

So that when you return to be king we might be your advisors." /A

Gilgamesh spoke to Enkidu, so that his voice might be heard, /A

"My friend, let us go to the grand palace of the queen Ninsun, /A

She is one who is filled with wisdom, all-seeing, all-knowing, /A

She will set the strong foundation of insight beneath our feet." /A

Thus they took hands and went off to Ninsun's grand palace /A

Gilgamesh rose and went into **the presence of his wise mother,** /A

"Mother, I am firm that I will travel upon the road to Humbaba /A

I am willing to face an unknown danger, to ride a forsaken path /A

Until the day comes when, after a long and perilous journey, /A

I will enter the Pine Forest and vanquish Humbaba, the terrible, /A

To wipe out from the world forever a demon Shamash despises /A

28

Humbaba's voice roars like the storm-surge, his speech is fire,　/(A)

His breath is death to man, he can hear as far as sixty leagues,　/(A)

Through the depths of the wood, might we trespass his forest?　/(A)

Ellil has made his sentinel Humbaba to be a terror to mankind　/(A)

Anyone who found his way through would surely meet his end　/(A)

Unless he who set forth was under the protection of some god　/-

And it is for this reason that we have come to be here with you."　/A

So Ninsun listened to every word spoken by her son Gilgamesh　/A

Then she entered into her private room for ritual purification　/A

She washed herself fully in water impregnated with tamarisk　/A

Clad herself in a fine robe which draped over all her contours　/A

And took a gold pendant as the sole decoration of her breast,　/A

With bracelets upon her arms and a tiara set upon her head　/A

Then enwrapping herself entirely within a full billowing cape　/-

When she was entirely ready she then made her way to the roof　/A

There presenting herself to Shamash, with an offering of smoke,　/A

And a disperse-offering to Shamash, raising her arms she spoke,　/A

"For what reason did you give Gilgamesh such a restless nature,　/A

By so doing my son is now set upon taking the road to Humbaba,　/A

By which he will face an unknown danger, ride a forsaken path　/A

Until the day comes when, after a long and perilous journey,　/A

He will enter the Pine Forest and vanquish Humbaba, the terrible,　/A

To wipe out from the world forever a demon whom you despise　/A

So during the day, as you pass from one side of earth to the other,　/A

May your bride Aya not be so daunted that he'd be left forsaken   /A

Rather let him be watched over by guardian angels of the night!   /A

You, Shamash, are the one who makes life flourish in the lands   /A

You, Lord, are the savior and guardian of the living upon earth   /-

Before your coming, O Shamash, was only night in this world,   /-

And every creature lived in fear in the dark, in perpetual terror   /-

It was you, Shamash, who opened the gates to let out the cattle,[*]   /A

For in those early days, you first arose for the sake of the earth   /A

When the high mountains were formed, the sky became bright,   /A

And all the wild animals were delighted by your brilliant light   /A

O Shamash, every day you are the one who rules over the world   /-

When you arise, your fire extinguishes the other fires of heaven   /-

And the entirety of humanity calls out in praise to you, Shamash,   /-

The world which desires your illumination calls for your coming,   /-

Man prays aloft to you, his voice is nothing more than a whisper   /-

He calls upon you when his kin are nowhere near, his dwelling far   /-

With the appearance of your brilliance all are brought together   /A

Even the Anunnaki, the high gods, anticipate your coming glow   /A

So during the day, as you pass from one side of earth to the other,   /A

May your bride Aya not be so daunted that he'd be left forsaken   /A

Rather let him be watched over by guardian angels of the night!   /A

Great Shamash, you must guard him when in his greatest peril   /-

Mighty Shamash, you must guide him when he faces his destiny   /-

And while Gilgamesh completes his journey to the Pine Forest   /(A)

---

[*] In the Vedas, the cattle released from the mountain by Indra were symbolic of the light of dawn.

Tablet III

Let the skies over his head not be overcast, but the days be bright   /-

Also make his way plain, that he won't stray from the true path   /-

And while Gilgamesh completes his journey to the Pine Forest   /A

May the days be of greater length and the nights pass quickly   /A

May he always have clothes to wear, and his pace **never falter**   /A

After sunset, may he always find a place to camp for the night   /A

And may the predators of the twilight **never come near to him**   /A

May your bride Aya not be so daunted that he'd be left forsaken   /A

And upon the day that Gilgamesh and Enkidu meet Humbaba,   /A

Shamash, stir up against Humbaba the thirteen raging winds: /A

The South Wind, the North Wind, East Wind, and West Wind   /A

Then call up the howling wind, gale-force wind, the arid wind,   /A

Then call up the terror gust, the humid wind, the frigid squall,   /A

Then call up the raging storm, tempest, and whipping tornado   /A

Let these thirteen winds be stirred up and Humbaba grow bleak   /A

Such that the weapons of Gilgamesh will prevail over Humbaba!   /A

And at dawn, when your own fire has been sparked once again,   /A

Then, Shamash, turn your attention to the one who serves you   /A

And then your swift-paced chargers will carry you on your way   /A

To a place of rest, where that night a bed will be readied for you   /A

While your kinsmen, the gods, will serve up your favorite dishes   /A

And your bride Aya will mop dry the drops from your forehead."   /A

Then once again the wild cow Ninsun made her plea to Shamash,   /A

"Shamash, is not Gilgamesh destined to find his way to the gods?   /A

Is he not fated to one day live within the heavens amongst you?   /A

31

Is he not fated to have a rod and a crown, just as the moon does? /A

Is he not fated to become as wise as Ea who dwells in the Abyss? /A

Is he not fated to rule over all people on earth along with Irnina?[*] /A

Is he not fated to live with Ningishzida in the Land of the Dead? /A

So I will now dedicate him **to you,** Shamash, **to assure his status** /A

In case **he meets doom on the way, or perishes** in the Pine Forest." /A

Once the wild cow Ninsun had beseeched Shamash in this way, /A

The wild cow Ninsun, filled with wisdom, all-seeing, all-knowing, /A

The wise mother of Gilgamesh, now concluded her appeals, /A

Then doused the smoke offering, **and descended from the roof,** /A

Summoning Enkidu to her that she might relate her thoughts, /A

"Although you are not my child, Enkidu, you are yet powerful /A

But from now on your descendants **will be wards of the temple,** /A

Under the care of the deaconesses and priestesses of Gilgamesh."[†] /A

With this she decorated him with a necklace charmed with sigils /A

"You have been taken in as an orphan by the dedicated matrons /A

You have been adopted into the care of the daughters of the gods /A

I accept Enkidu as my son, who will now be Gilgamesh's **brother** /A

Also **may your way be plain, that you not stray from the true path** /A

And while you complete your journey together to the Pine Forest /A

May the days be of greater length and the nights pass quickly /A

May you always have clothes to wear, and your pace **never falter** /A

---

[*] Irnina is essentially identical to Ishtar, goddess of love and war

[†] The descendants of Enkidu, meaning orphans, like himself.

After sunset, may you always find a place to camp for the night   /A

And may **you have** protection **from all predators of the twilight**   /A

And may Shamash preserve you on your way to the Pine Forest   /A[16]

Whether it be a month **or ten months**, a year **or even ten years."**   /A

Then the wise mother of Gilgamesh, who knew all, now spoke,   /(A)

The untamed heifer Ninsun, who knew all, said to Gilgamesh,   /(A)

"Please the god with incense offerings and make him a promise   /-

Fulfill that promise when you return, and you have met success   /-

And return with pine wood fit for a door to decorate his temple.   /-

Now go, Gilgamesh, **to the temple of Shamash, to make offerings**   /A

At **his temple, standing as a beacon at the very heart of the city."**   /A

So the two brothers took hands and went through the Pine Gate   /A

In the Shrine of Shamash Enkidu **brought offerings to the god,**   /A

In the Shrine of Shamash Gilgamesh **brought gifts for the god:**   /A

They brought incense of juniper, **tamarisk, cedar, and cypress**   /A

Around them flocked the members of the **priesthood of Shamash**   /A

They gave assistance to the pair, aided in preparing the offering   /-

And Enkidu raised his voice to be heard and spoke to Gilgamesh,   /-

"You should be most concerned now about keeping yourself safe   /-

If **you pray** to **your god then let him set** you **on the straight path**   /B

Have him persuade you to take the road back to the safe haven   /B

Have him cause you to find your way back to the wide city, Uruk."   /B

Then Gilgamesh, kneeling **before the god,** spoke **in prayer to him,**   /B

"I will proceed on! And Shamash **you will assure me of victory**   /B

Guarantee my preservation, lead me unhurt to the safe haven   /B

Assure to me that you will bring about my protection hereafter." /B

Gilgamesh called out **that his voice might be heard, to the priests** /B

And at his command **they then brought in the required presents** /B

They made offerings of juniper wood and incense upon the altar /-

And they pledged to return with wood fit for a door for his temple /-

When he would fructify them in their action against Humbaba /-

Should they be victorious against the demon Shamash despises /-

Then the city elders gave their blessing, speaking to Gilgamesh, /B

"May Shamash cause you to win in your glorious confrontation /B

So that you will see with your own eyes what you have prayed for /B

That he will breach the barricade, sweep clear the road for you /B

That he make mountain ways plain, and fill your heart with joy /B

Then at night,* might you find Lugalbanda to be your guardian /B

He will stand near you at your victory, which shall be child's play /B

According to the will of Shamash you shall fulfill **your purpose** /A

After walking through Marduk's Gate, **then continue to the west** /A

And follow thereafter the course of the waters **of the Euphrates** /A

On your return **you can construct a boat to make your way back** /A

Within it the pine door will not **be difficult to transport to Sippar** /A

Gilgamesh **will be guardian to his friend and fend off all threats** /A

Enkidu **will lead you on your way to the edge of the Pine Forest** /A

After going a distance of 20 leagues then eat some of your food, /A

Be sure to wash off your feet in Humbaba's river, as you planned /B

---

* Shamash is the sun and thus can only watch over Gilgamesh during the daylight hours.

Be sure to dig out a pit when you halt to camp during the night   /B

Assure that your water-skins are never without drinkable water   /B

Pour out water to Shamash, and save a prayer for Lugalbanda."   /B

Then Gilgamesh, the King of Uruk, addressed the city officials,   /-

"We are firm that we shall travel upon the road to Humbaba   /(A)

And are willing to face unknown danger, to ride a forsaken path   /(A)

Until the day comes when, after a long and perilous journey,   /A

We enter the Pine Forest and vanquish Humbaba, the terrible,   /A

To wipe out from the world forever a demon Shamash despises   /A

You men of distinction, do not let falter the preservation of law   /-

And let none of you gain anything **which is not rightfully yours**   /A

The officials are forbidden from amassing young men in the city   /A

But they are to be judges in matters of law, and to assure justice   /A

While we are off achieving our victory, which shall be child's play   /A

While we are propelling our blades deep into Humbaba's heart!"   /A

The officials stood around him and gave him their well-wishes,   /A

While Uruk's young men followed behind him in a multitude   /A

The officials kissed his feet, **then the they spoke to Gilgamesh,**   /A, B

"Heed us that you might come back to the safe haven of Uruk   /A

Gilgamesh, be not so bold to trust only in your physical might   /A

After giving your eyes time to judge, trust in your first stroke   /A

He who leads on the path will be the one who saves his friend   /A

The one well familiar with the ways will be his brother's savior   /A

Thus allow Enkidu to lead the way, he's familiar with the routes   /A

He knows how to fight and can provide you good battle advice   /A

He has often traversed the mountains, walked upon far ridges,　　/A

So let Enkidu be a guardian to his friend and preserve your life　　/A

That you might come back safely, to return and satisfy brides,　　/A

So that we who advise might rely upon you to remain our king,　　/A

So that when you return to be king we might be your advisors."　　/A

And Enkidu raised his voice to be heard and spoke to Gilgamesh,　　/A

"Change your mind now, my friend, it is not yet too late for us　　/A

The journey which is not begun is one which need not be finished　　/A

We can still put aside our arms and abandon this fateful quest　　/-

If we halt and return, people will think no less of you than now."　　/-

Gilgamesh listened to everything Enkidu had said, then spoke,　　/-

When Gilgamesh spoke to Enkidu, tears were upon his cheeks,　　/B

"Should I rather think then about the quest I refrained from?　　/B

Has not my god already the knowledge of what is to come?　　/B

Am I destined that I will forever be safe and secure in my life?　　/B

Will I find my greatest bliss in mere festivity and gratification?　　/B

To be content to live so we might enjoy each others company?　　/B

Is life best experienced from just being seated upon thrones?"　　/B

So then Gilgamesh went to gather together his warrior's gear　　/B

They took up their sizeable blades, picked up a bow and quiver　　/B

Outfitted themselves for a war, pulled gloves over their hands　　/B

Then Gilgamesh raised the double-bladed axe within his hand　　/B

He put his Anshan-fashioned bow and quiver over his shoulder　　/B

Pointed the sword downward and sheathed the blade on his belt　　/B

Tablet III

Then the two of them were prepared to set forth on their quest   /B

The daughters-in-law were led to the side of Gilgamesh, saying,   /B

"When will you come back to us, returning here to Uruk's walls?"   /B

Then Enkidu raised his voice to be heard, speaking to Gilgamesh,   /B

"There will be many things which will frighten you on your way   /B

Just realize that there is no reason to be scared, but follow me   /B

Yet the way there is perilous, his abode shadowed in darkness   /B

Take no servants with you, or they'll stray from the road we go   /B

Tell them that they cannot come with you, so order them home."   /B

And Gilgamesh raised his voice to be heard, speaking to Enkidu,   /-[17]

"There is no reason I can see as to why they need accompany me,   /B

So you are free to return to my palace, so I'll say farewell to you."[*]   /B

The servants of Gilgamesh were glad upon hearing him say this   /B

Then the young men **of Uruk gathered to make their farewells,**   /B

"Go to your victory, Gilgamesh, and may Shamash be **with you."**   /B

And so Gilgamesh and Enkidu **raised their final parting waves**   /B

As they set off together, with the crowd of Uruk watching them,   /-

Gilgamesh spoke out, raised his voice that he might be heard,   /-

"Upon your oath give assurance that you will keep my city secure   /-

And that it will be blessed with peace and order until I return,   /-

So now may I at last go to see this demon whose voice resounds,   /B[18]

Who bears the name which the ravines of the valley forever echo   /B

That I may now make my way to the Pine Forest, to defeat him,   /B

So that all the lands know just how mighty the child of Uruk is!   /B

---

[*] In the Sumerian version a retinue of his servants do accompany them.

I will go to work and fell lofty pines, and enjoy eternal renown!"   /B

And as they walked the shouts from the city walls slowly faded   /-

There lingered within his deepest thoughts voices heard before,   /-

"Gilgamesh, you are still young and although you are now eager,   /(A)

You have no idea what adversities you will find upon your quest   /(A)

Humbaba's voice roars like the storm-surge, his speech is fire,   /(A)

His breath is death to man, he can hear as far as sixty leagues   /(A)

Through the depths of the wood, who could trespass his forest?   /(A)

Anyone who found his way through would surely meet his end   /(A)

Who even among the gods would be able to stand against him?   /(A)

Ellil has made his sentinel Humbaba to be a terror to mankind   /(A)

Gilgamesh, be not so bold to trust only in your physical might   /A[19]

After giving your eyes time to judge, trust in your first stroke   /A

He who leads on the path will be the one who saves his friend   /A

The one well familiar with the ways will be his brother's savior   /A

Thus allow Enkidu to lead the way, he's familiar with the routes   /A

He knows how to fight and can provide you good battle advice   /A

So let Enkidu be a guardian to his friend and preserve your life   /(A)

That you might come back safely, to return and satisfy brides,   /(A)

So that we who advise might rely upon you to remain our king,   /(A)

So that when you return to be king we might be your advisors."   /(A)

(The two of them traversed the way, as Enkidu led them forward)

TABLET IV

The two of them traversed the way, as Enkidu led them forward /-
On the path which would lead them to the edge of the Pine Forest /-
Walking along the ridge, guided by the passage of the Euphrates /-
After going a distance of 20 leagues they ate what food they had /A
After going for 30 leagues they stopped to camp for the night /A
Then during the day they went on until they had gone 50 leagues /A
In the duration of new moon to full moon and three days more, /A
Arrived in Lebanon, digging a hole in the ground before the sun /A
They refilled their water-skins and poured out a libation to him /A
Gilgamesh went by himself up the mountain with an offering, /A
Leaving flour for **the spirits of the mountain, then prayed to it**, /A
"O mountain, send to me a dream and one full of good fortune!" /A
Enkidu took care of things for Gilgamesh, erecting a dream tent /A[*]
Such that when a wind-devil entered, he covered over the door /A
And forced it to lie flat within a circle **he'd scored on the ground** /A
Setting it down like wild barley, **he hacked it, spilling its** blood /A
Gilgamesh himself sat there resting his chin upon his knees, /A
Until sleep, which spreads itself over humanity, overcame him /A
In the middle of the watch he awoke and told his companion, /A
"My brother, if you did not call me then why am I now awake? /A

---

[*] These four lines remain difficult to interpret, especially given their fragmented state, but they essentially amount to the performance of a ritual to elicit prophetic dreams. A similar metaphor is used here as in the Sumerian "Battle of the Hero" concerning the Bull of Heaven.

If you did not touch me, then why is it I am in such distress?　/A

If a divinity did not go past, then why is my flesh quivering?　/A

Friend, **I had a dream** and it was a dream that was disturbing　/A

We were standing at the foot of a mountain, **looming over us,**　/A

Then the mountain peak came crashing down, and buried us　/A

In relationship to its size we were like flies **compared to a bull."**　/A

He who understood, the one who was born in the wilderness,　/A

Enkidu heard and then interpreted the dream for Gilgamesh,　/A

"My friend your dream is a propitious one, of great importance,　/A

For the mountain that you saw **falling on us was not Humbaba,**　/A

Rather we will strike him down and cast his body into a cesspit　/A

When dawn rises we will hear the favorable words of Shamash."　/A

After going a distance of 20 leagues they ate what food they had　/A

After going for 30 leagues they stopped to camp for the night　/A

Then during the day they went on until they had gone 50 leagues　/A

In the duration of new moon to full moon and three days more,　/A

They set about digging a hole in the ground before Shamash　/A

They refilled their water-skins and poured out a libation to him　/A

Gilgamesh went by himself up the mountain with an offering,　/A

Leaving flour for **the spirits of the mountain, then prayed to it,**　/A

"O mountain, send to me a dream and one full of good fortune!"　/(A)

Enkidu took care of things for Gilgamesh, erecting a dream tent　/(A)

Such that when a wind-devil entered, he covered over the door　/(A)

And forced it to lie flat within a circle he'd scored on the ground　/(A)

Tablet IV

Setting it down like wild barley, he hacked it, spilling its blood	/A
Gilgamesh himself sat there resting his chin upon his knees,	/(A)
Until sleep, which spreads itself over humanity, overcame him	/(A)
In the middle of the watch he awoke and told his companion,	/(A)
"My brother, if you did not call me then why am I now awake?	/(A)
If you did not touch me, then why is it I am in such distress?	/(A)
If a divinity did not go past, then why is my flesh quivering?	/(A)
Friend, I had another dream and one even more distressing	/(A)
I saw a raging tidal flood which was topping, about to crash	/-[20]
Then an intense light flashed and the flood waters evaporated	/-
And a thousand boulders fell out of the sky and into the ocean	/-
They crashed down creating a horrendous din of dire calamity	/-
Until the entire ocean was filled and I could no longer see it."	/-
He who understood, the one who was born in the wilderness,	/(A)
Enkidu heard and then interpreted the dream for Gilgamesh,	/(A)
"My friend your dream is a propitious one, of great importance,	/A
Humbaba was like **a tidal mount which was rearing up over us**	/A[*]

---

[*] A Middle Babylonian Hittite version of the second dream is somewhat different:

> The second dream I had is one even more ominous than the first
>
> In this dream, my good friend, there was a high mountain **peak**
>
> It fell, tossing me down, trapping my feet, **and would not let go**
>
> Then shone a great light that became brighter, and a man **came**
>
> No man could be more striking anywhere, his looks **outshone all**
>
> He pulled me **from** beneath this tidal mount and **drew me clear**
>
> He provided water to quench my thirst, and I felt fully **restored**

41

But a beam of light shone out **from there and made him falter**   /A
Then we set upon him the **boulders fallen from mountaintops**   /A
Feeling a rage of fury towards Humbaba, **we would not relent**   /A
Then when we had finished we stood there looking down at him   /A
When dawn rises we will hear the favorable words of Shamash."   /A

After going a distance of 20 leagues they ate what food they had   /A
After going for 30 leagues they stopped to camp for the night   /A
Then during the day they went on until they had gone 50 leagues   /A
They set about digging a hole in the ground before Shamash   /A
They refilled their water-skins and poured out a libation to him   /A
Gilgamesh went by himself up the mountain with an offering,   /A
Leaving flour for **the spirits of the mountain, and he prayed to it**,   /A
"O mountain, send to me a dream and one full of good fortune!"   /A
Enkidu took care of things for Gilgamesh, erecting a dream tent   /A
Such that when a wind-devil entered, he covered over the door   /A
And forced it to lie flat within a circle **he'd scored on the ground**   /A
Setting it down like wild barley, **he hacked it, spilling its** blood   /A
Gilgamesh himself sat there resting his chin upon his knees   /A
Until sleep, which spreads itself over humanity, overcame him   /A

And then he helped me to get me back upon **my two** feet again."
Enkidu heard and then interpreted the dream for Gilgamesh,
"My friend, we will **not face a mountain,** he is entirely different,
Humbaba, **guardian of the Pine Forest,** was not the mountain
He is entirely different; **therefore,** you should not be concerned

Tablet IV

In the middle of the watch he awoke and told his companion,   /A

"My brother, if you did not call me then why am I now awake?   /A

If you did not touch me, then why is it I am in such distress?   /A

If a divinity did not go past, then why is my flesh quivering?   /A

Friend, I had another dream and one even more distressing   /A

The sky was screeching with a shrill cry, the very earth roared   /A

The sounds of the day were silenced, and a looming dark grew   /A

There was lightning which flared from the sky, igniting fires   /A

The flames burned noisily beneath, deathly ash cascaded down   /A

The flashing was diminished and the flames were quenched   /A

The dark ashes which were falling became shimmering embers."   /A

He who understood, the one who was born in the wilderness,   /A

Enkidu heard everything, to tell him what it meant, and spoke,   /A

"My friend your dream is a propitious one, of great importance,   /A

"You saw the earth and heaven which were both in an upheaval   /-[21]

With all sound and sights of the world at once extinguished,   /-

The flaming fires and the ashes of death were an ominous sign   /-

The sparking which was ignited had been quenched by death   /-

But this could only mean the looming death facing Humbaba,   /-

It could only be a sign that we will relentlessly bring him down   /-

Because there is no surer indication that destruction is at hand."   /-*

---

* A section from the Old Babylonian version contains something concerning their approach to the Pine

Forest, when Enkidu says to Gilgamesh:

"My friend, as we come ever nearer and nearer to the Pine Forest,

Our expectations will soon be realized, and conflict draws near

43

The Gilgamesh Cycle

After going a distance of 20 leagues they ate what food they had	/A
After going for 30 leagues they stopped to camp for the night	/A
Then during the day they went on until they had gone 50 leagues	/A
They set about digging a hole in the ground before Shamash	/A
They refilled their water-skins and poured out a libation to him	/A
Gilgamesh went by himself up the mountain with an offering,	/A
Leaving flour for **the spirits of the mountain, and he prayed to it**,	/A
"O mountain, send to me a dream and one full of good fortune!"	/A
Enkidu took care of things for Gilgamesh, erecting a dream tent	/A
Such that when a wind-devil entered, he covered over the door	/A
And forced it to lie flat within a circle **he'd scored on the ground**	/A
Setting it down like wild barley, **he hacked it**, **spilling its** blood	/A
Gilgamesh himself sat there resting his chin upon his knees	/A
Until sleep, which spreads itself over humanity, overcame him	/A
In the middle of the watch he awoke and told his companion,	/A
"My brother, if you did not call me then why am I now awake?	/A
If you did not touch me, then why is it I am in such distress?	/A
If a divinity did not go past, then why is my flesh quivering?	/A
Friend, I had another dream and one even more distressing	/A
And by my reckoning it is one far worse than the other three	/B

You will first perceive divine Humbaba's Mantles of Brilliance

Then in a contest like that between two bulls with horns locked,

You will strike him, and make his head bow down by your might

But the elder gentleman you saw, he is the god who guards you

This one is the very father who sired you, Lugalbanda the divine."

There was an Anzu-bird rising through the sky, like a cloud   /B

And it circled directly over us, but its appearance was unusual   /B

And flames were being emitted from its beak, expelling death   /B

Likewise there was also a figure, and he too was unusual to see   /B

Of great proportions, just as I saw him standing in the dream   /B

And he bound it by its wings, then he took hold of my hand,   /B

And pulled the Anzu-bird from the sky and threw it at my feet   /B

After, both he and I then stamped our feet upon it, **crushing it.**"   /B

Enkidu heard everything, to tell him what it meant, and spoke,   /B

"There was an Anzu-bird rising through the sky, like a cloud   /B

And it circled directly over us, but its appearance was unusual   /B

And flames were being emitted from its beak, expelling death   /B

Thus at first you shall feel fear at Humbaba's awesome powers   /B

But then I will draw it down by its feet and you shall conquer!   /B

And the figure you saw, this was great Shamash, our guardian   /B

My friend your dream is a propitious one, of great importance,   /B

Friend, we will not face this **Anzu-bird, he is entirely different,**   /B

Here we have Humbaba compared to **the weakened Anzu-bird**   /B

Shamash's powers will rise **against him and prevail** against him   /B

We will cause him to be brought down, and pinion its pinions,   /B

He will be held and we shall **not be in any danger from its talons**   /B

His **feet will be hacked off and then** we will trod upon his body   /B

When dawn rises we will hear the favorable words of Shamash."   /(A)

After going a distance of 20 leagues they ate what food they had   /A

After going for 30 leagues they stopped to camp for the night   /A

Then during the day they went on until they had gone 50 leagues   /A

They set about digging a hole in the ground before Shamash   /A

They refilled their water-skins and poured out a libation to him   /A

Gilgamesh went by himself up the mountain with an offering,   /A

Leaving flour for **the spirits of the mountain, and he prayed to it**,   /A

"O mountain, send to me a dream and one full of good fortune!"   /A

Enkidu took care of things for Gilgamesh, erecting a dream tent   /A

Such that when a wind-devil entered, he covered over the door   /A

And forced it to lie flat within a circle **he'd scored on the ground**   /A

Setting it down like wild barley, **he hacked it, spilling its** blood   /A

Gilgamesh himself sat there resting his chin upon his knees   /A

Until sleep, which spreads itself over humanity, overcame him   /A

In the middle of the watch he awoke and told his companion,   /A

"My brother, if you did not call me then why am I now awake?   /A

If you did not touch me, then why is it I am in such distress?   /A

If a divinity did not go past, then why is my flesh quivering?   /A

Friend, I had another dream and one even more distressing   /A

In it I grappled with a wild buffalo, which bellowed up a storm,   /B

And the plumes of dust it sent forth went high into the heavens   /B

There I was, standing before it, when it reached forth its hands   /B

It grabbed **my neck with one hand,** taking my arm **with the other**   /B

Then a man came to release me **from the bull,** pulling me **away**   /B

My cheeks **were sunken and** my **mouth was parched from thirst**   /B

So *he provided me* water from his water-skin **that I might drink.**" /B
(Enkidu heard and then interpreted the dream for Gilgamesh,)
"My friend, the **divine being** we face is not the wild bull you saw, /B
He is entirely different; rather the buffalo was brilliant Shamash, /B
It is he who will take our hands and guide us in our challenge /B
While the other who provided water to drink from his water-skin /B
That was rather the god who esteems you, Lugalbanda the divine /B
So shall we work together to achieve what has not been tried /B
To perform a deed never seen, and unmatched in all the world!" /B

They went on from there until they reached the mountain pass /-
They made their camp for the night, and lay themselves down /-
Then heard the beasts in the high passes, starting to assemble /-
Gilgamesh perceived them first, then distinguished their shapes /-
It was a pride of hungry mountain lions, and they frightened him /-
Gilgamesh could do nothing for the sake of saving his friend /-
He looked without moving, standing without his knees shifting /-
He remained too fearful to go out against them, he was terrified /-
So he lifted up his eyes to make a prayer to Sin, heaven's lantern, /(A)
"Oh great lord Sin, as you look upon me now, preserve me now!" /-
Enkidu, who had gone to sleep, was startled out of his dream /(A)
When he leapt up he was greatly possessed of a fervent instinct /(A)
And he grasped the axe beside him, and unsheathed his sword /(A)
As fast as a dart he quickly leapt among them and took them on /(A)
Enkidu looked and saw Gilgamesh was not moving to aid him /-

Enkidu raised his voice to be heard, to his brother Gilgamesh, /-

"Why do you remain there unmoving, doing nothing but gazing /-

Are you standing in your sleep, do you think you are dreaming? /-

We will do a great deal better if we engage them as partners, /-

We will do far more harm to them if we were to work together." /-

There he gave blows with his weapons, and smashed their skulls /-

The following day he went out, standing before Shamash at noon /-

And he gave the bodies of the lions to him as a thank offering /-

He carved out their hearts, offering them to the spirits by name /-

Then he spoke to Shamash, giving him thanks for his aid, saying, /-

"O Shamash, every day you are the one who rules over the world /-

When you arise, your fire extinguishes the other fires of heaven /-

And the entirety of humanity calls out in praise to you, Shamash, /-

The world which desires your illumination calls for your coming, /-

Man prays aloft to you, his voice is nothing more than a whisper /-

He calls upon you when his kin are nowhere near, his dwelling far /-

O mighty Shamash, through the strength you gave me did we live /-

Now are these dedicated to you for bringing us into your service /-

May your light never be shed from our heads, and preserve us." /-

Then Enkidu raised his voice to be heard, speaking to Gilgamesh, /-

"Gilgamesh you have mislaid your courage upon this bleak tract /-

When you boasted that you would prevail against any foe before /-

Why did you refrain, for the man-eaters are nothing like cattle? /-

Without the mighty wall of Uruk to protect you, you must rise up /-

Just as though the wild beasts were but like any other combatants /-

48

You got used to prevailing against others, you became arrogant /-
But when you faced these you were so afraid you could not move /-
Petrified with fright when you stood face to face with their ferocity /-
They knew nothing of your greatness, did not cower in fear of you /-
So you will find yourself sometime, when you can't help yourself /-
I swear you will lose something dear to you, from your cowardice." /-
Then Enkidu spoke so that his voice might be heard, to Gilgamesh, /-
"Had I not been dreaming I would not have been so aggravated /-
What I saw was enough to wake me up during my slumbering /-
But when I saw the lions I was immediately overcome by instinct /-
That I rushed in the middle of the pride without thinking twice /-
And I was fearful for the safety of my brother, so that I attacked /-
Yet this dream I had was not so favorable for either you or me /-
In it you were in a frightful state, wandering only in a lion-skin /-
But it was even more ominous for me, for I was not at your side /-
But you carried in your arms my weapons, my own sword and axe /-
Then you threw them down and buried them beneath the ground /-
Crying over them as though they were your dearest companion." /-
Enkidu had been scraped by the lion's sharp claws, his flesh torn /-
Seeking from amongst the plants, Enkidu found a healing herb /-
Smearing it onto himself, he utilized this to salve his own wounds /-
And he also gave it to Gilgamesh, that he might gain its benefit /-
But the foreboding of death was eroding Enkidu's spirit to fight, /-
Enkidu spoke to Gilgamesh so that his voice might be heard, /A
"How could I now enter the Pine Forest and cut through a trail, /A

How could I open a way when my arms are now so weakened?"   /A

Gilgamesh spoke to Enkidu so that his voice might be heard,   /A

"Why friend do we now speak of hesitation like the cowardly?   /A

We still might first cross over all the mountains, **then we'll see**   /A

Before we face **the Pine Forest** and need to start felling trees,   /A

My brother, you know conflict and have learned to fight well   /A

You have protected your skin with herbs that you might not fall   /A

You will shine **like the sun** in a double-thick Mantle of Brilliance   /A

You will give out a war cry akin to the crash of kettle drums   /A

You will find weakness will no longer be lingering in your limbs   /A

You will find weakness will no longer be lingering at your loins   /A

Come with me, take my hand, friend, and we shall go together   /A

Your heart and soul will soon be eager for the fever of battle,   /A

Do not think at a time like this of death, but think only of life   /A

Man is both worthy and able in battle, looking out for his friend   /A

For if he moves ahead of him and defends him, he will be safe   /A

And by doing such will have secured fame for all of eternity."   /A

So encouraged now by these words, the two arrived together   /A

Merely looking out from where they stood, at a loss for words   /A

(They remained there at the forest's edge, just gazing upon it)

TABLET V

They remained there at the forest's edge, just gazing upon it /A

They regarded the sheer height of the pines and the approach /A

The trail that Humbaba had made when he went to and fro /A

The ways were well worn and the road was exceptionally good /A

From there they could see Pine Mountain, home of the gods /A

The trees were abundant right up the sides of the mountain /A

Casting a fine shade which filled their spirits with serene joy /A

And with rampant undergrowth twining through the wood /A

Interspersed throughout it were a bewildering variety of trees /-[22]

After a moment's hesitation, they proceeded on the good path /-

They walked from there, continuing through mountain passes /-

They made their camp for the night, and lay themselves down /-

Then heard the beasts in the high passes, starting to assemble /-

Gilgamesh perceived them first, then distinguished their shapes /-

It was a pride of hungry mountain lions, and they frightened him /-

But Gilgamesh rose up with trembling for the sake of his friend /-

And when his friend rose up beside him, his own fear diminished /-

Then they took up their weapons, and shook one another's hand /-

As fast as a dart they leapt among the lions and took them on /-

Together they struck blows with their daggers, making them fall /A

Then lifted their swords from sheathes, killing every one of them /A

After hacking them apart, their axes were now covered in blood /A

So both hatchets and daggers were in need of being sharpened /A

51

One of them holding while the other polished it with the stone /A

Then they made their way into the woods near Humbaba's lair /A

But Humbaba was no longer far distant, no longer a fairy tale /A

As they went on his tracks could be seen, wide with clawed toes /-

In the distance they could see his glowing Mantles of Brilliance /-

Enkidu felt the real presence of doom, and he stopped his trek /-

And Gilgamesh spoke that his voice might be heard, to Enkidu, /A

"What troubles you, my friend, that you are reluctant to go on /A

You must not be fearful of your evil dream, for I know better now /-

Your dream was singular, the portent dire, your grief quite plain, /(A)

The portent was dire, your dream was singular, your grief plain, /(A)

Enough to cause the heart-strain they bring to continue for a year /(A)

Your dream caused a heart-strain which will be felt into next year /(A)

But you alone were able to drive away the lions without assistance /-

And just see what we are capable of doing when we work together, /-

For although Ellil made Humbaba fearsome, he is not immortal." /A

Enkidu raised up his voice to be heard, and spoke to Gilgamesh, /A

"My friend, you know Humbaba is the worst sort of fire-demon /A

But once you see him in person, you too will not be so confident." /A

And Gilgamesh spoke that his voice might be heard, to Enkidu, /A

"A lone person hasn't someone to lift him up nor to cover his back /A

Those he encounters he does not know, he being at their mercy /A

The way is treacherous, for the one alone knows not whom to trust /A

However when two lay down they are warm, him he can rely upon /A

Two together can succeed when the one man would be overcome /A

The rope with three-strands is the most difficult to break in two[*]   /A

Even the strongest of lions **is not able to overcome** two lesser ones   /A

With two of us we have an endurance which will bring us victory   /-[23]

Surely we shall, both of us, prevail against the demon Humbaba."   /-

Enkidu raised up his voice to be heard, and spoke to Gilgamesh,   /(A)

"Here we find ourselves where a man's feet ought not to tread,   /B

So let us rather abandon our weapons here at Humbaba's gate!"   /B

Then Enkidu spoke again, stating this to his friend, **Gilgamesh,**   /B

"Humbaba is like a storm-surge, and like Adad he will crush us."   /B

Then Gilgamesh spoke that his voice might be heard, to Enkidu,   /(A)

"Then let us clear away the gloom, and bring light into the wood   /-

We'll bring the trees down and allow radiant Shamash to shine!"   /-

So they took up their iron-axes and began hacking tree trunks   /-

They struck at each one with vigor, until it came angling down   /-

And Shamash's vibrant beams penetrated the forest darkness   /-

The sound of the thundering crash reverberated throughout   /-

The echoes fed straight through into the deep lair of Humbaba   /-

Picked up by his keen ears, they, able to discern a distant whisper,   /-

Were aggravated by the clatter that kept up and grew louder   /-

---

[*] These lines are partly reconstructed utilizing Ecclesiastes 4:9-12, which reads:

"Two are superior to one as they will have success in their work. If one of them falls the other will pick him up; but sorry is the one who walks alone, for when he falls he lacks someone to bring him to his feet. Just so, when two lie down they will keep warm together, but can a man stay warm if he is alone? One man can easily overcome the man who walks alone, whereas two can fight him off. The cord of three stands is not so readily split."

He sensed what was making its way through could be a menace /-
But there could be no men who would be so bold as to do this /-
When even the high gods would not provoke such a challenge /-
Gilgamesh and Enkidu struck trunks until their muscles ached /-
But each was driven on even more by the fortitude of his brother /-
Together they cleared a gap, struck away the looming darkness /-
Until the pathway they were making broke through to a clearing /-
And there enshrouded in a thick cloud was the demon waiting /-
Now they were there, the dwelling looked as bad as it could have, /-
With his form ten times more menacing than could be imagined /-
They held their ground more out of shock than from courage /-
As they stood with axes fallen, there face to face with the demon /-

Humbaba spoke to Gilgamesh that his voice might be heard, /L
"This fool should ask himself why he brought this brute to me, /L
His friend is a shrimp who does not even know his own father! /L
So small, in fact, that to me he is nothing more than a turtle /L
Who did not even take his mother's milk, thus why take notice /L
Even if I devoured him I think it would hardly satisfy my hunger /L
Why then, Gilgamesh, did you bring him within my reach? /L
While Enkidu stands there watching and waiting like a bandit /L
I would tear my teeth through his neck and sever his windpipe /L
Leaving his trunk for lions to gorge upon and birds to peck at." /L
Gilgamesh raised his voice that he might be heard, to Enkidu, /L
"My brother, Humbaba has now taken on a different aspect /L

Tablet V

And the **fierceness** which strengthens within him **is fearsome**	/L
Such that my heart quivers, as he at any moment **may strike!**"	/L
Enkidu raised his voice to be heard, and spoke to Gilgamesh,	/L
"My friend, for what reason do you chatter like the cowardly,	/L
Using words which are weak, and why do you shelter yourself?	/L
Now you see, my friend, that there is but one **thing we must do**	/L
Now that the copper is all ready for pouring down the channel	/L
Just an hour of working the bellows, just an hour **at the furnace**	/L
To unleash the Flood-weapon, and to strike with searing lashes!	/L
So do not fall back now, do not falter, retracing your own steps	/L
Rather resolve yourself to beat him by striking him even more!"	/L
At that Gilgamesh grabbed firmly his axe handle and moved in	/-
Making his first blow to count, striking where his vitals should be	/-
But the blade would not bite, the hardest blow was no menace	/-
With this he was shaken inside and beat a retreat away at once	/-
Making his way to an open space, left very weary and dejected	/-
He **fell upon his knees and** wept tears that fell before Shamash,	/A
"Do you recall what you had spoken when we were in Uruk,	/A
So remain where you are and hear everything I have to say."	/A
And Shamash listened to what Gilgamesh said, and replied,	/A
At that moment a booming voice addressed him from the sky, *	/(A)
"Then make your charge, stand against him, so he cannot retreat,	/A
To enter the forest for safety, to go deep into the wood, nor **flee**	/A
You will find that he will no longer be protected by seven mantles	/A

---

* Following Dalley (see Dalley 2000: 128)

But rather he will only have on one, for the other six will be gone   /A

And he will utter a bellowing roar as does the charging buffalo   /A

There will be but one bellow first, but it will be enough to terrify   /A

Humbaba, the forest's guardian, will then bellow **a second time**   /A

This will be enough to shake the trees, but still do not be shaken   /-

Humbaba will give a roar which will **boom like the thundercloud**   /A

Reverberating in the mountains, but this too you must endure."   /-[24]

So Gilgamesh approached Humbaba with his weapons raised   /-

He made his charge, stood against him, so he could not retreat,   /(A)

To enter the forest for safety, to go deep into the wood, nor flee   /(A)

Unable to go into the forest, back into the woods, he was beset   /-

Then he uttered a bellowing roar as does the charging buffalo   /-

There was but one bellow, enough to terrify, before a second   /-

It shook the trees, then the third boomed like the thundercloud   /-

Reverberating in the mountains, but this too Gilgamesh endured   /-

Then when the bronze blades **had been honed with fine edges,**   /A

They reached and took out of their scabbards **the sharp daggers**   /A

The blades were corroded **by the atmosphere of the dank woods**   /A

Their daggers and swords **and axes were all prepared for battle**   /A

One **of them holding while the other** polished it with the stone   /A

And they put on **their battle helmets and took up their war gear**   /A

Humbaba **watched their preparations, and grew keenly restless,**   /A

"He is not inclined to leave, **as they are making ready to battle**   /A

He is not inclined to leave, **but is willing to make his challenge**   /A

To the one guarding the Pine Forest, Ellil made terrible to man   /(A)

His voice roars like the storm-surge, his speech is a baleful fire /(A)

His breath is death to man, he can hear as far as sixty leagues /(A)

There is no way that man can contend, no way he might prevail /-

But if they did Ellil would hear of it, and the gods will not sit still /-

May Ellil call together the gods to unleash their fury upon them." /A

Enkidu raised up his voice to be heard, and spoke to Humbaba, /A

"A lone person hasn't someone to lift him up nor to cover his back /A

Those he encounters he does not know, he being at their mercy /A

The way is treacherous for the one alone knows not whom to trust /A

However when two lay down they are warm, him he can rely upon /A

Two together can succeed when the one man would be overcome /A

The rope with three-strands is the most difficult to break in two /A

Even the strongest of lions is not able to overcome two lesser ones /A

With two of us we have an endurance which will bring us victory /-

Surely we shall, both of us, prevail against the demon Humbaba." /-

So the two of them went forth and attacked now with their sabers /-

Cleaved the air with hard blades, cut the sky with sharp daggers /-

But the striking was ineffective, the full force of the weapons dull /-

Then Gilgamesh called out to Shamash, praying now for his aid /-

And he manifested himself, making his way straight to Humbaba /-

Raising up he lashed him in his torso, but each strike was parried /L

The ground upon which they tread with their heels was torn up /L

The lands of Sirara and Lebanon were ripped up by their shifting /L

The clouds darkened, ash enclosed around them as thick as fog /L

Then Shamash called to him the great winds to harass Humbaba /L

The South Wind, the North Wind, East Wind, and West Wind   /L

He called up the howling wind, gale-force wind, the arid wind,   /L

He called up the terror gust, the humid wind, the frigid squall,   /L

He called up the raging storm, tempest, and whipping tornado   /L

These thirteen winds were stirred up and Humbaba grew bleak   /L

He was unable to strike ahead of him but was unable to retreat   /L

So Gilgamesh's weapons were now made effective against him   /L

The power of the seven mantles faltered, each went its own way   /-

Until he was no longer protected by seven mantles, but only one   /-

As Humbaba was breathing heavily, he spoke to Gilgamesh,   /L

"Gilgamesh, you are but a youth, and were born from a mother   /L

You are one of **the gods**, made by Shamash, god of the mountain,   /L

You are the child of Uruk, you are Gilgamesh the King of Uruk   /L

Much there is to gain, Gilgamesh, which the dead cannot **bestow**   /L

Only the living **subject** can serve his lord, **and give him benefit**   /L

Spare me, Gilgamesh, and **I will enlarge your wealth with gifts,**   /L

And assure that they grow bountifully for you in **the Pine Forest**   /L

You will have as many trees as you **might wish from henceforth**   /L

The best of myrtle, **cedar, and pine which I will guard just for you**   /L

Wood timbers which will make **your** kingdom the envy of many."   /L

Enkidu raised up his voice to be heard, and spoke to Gilgamesh,   /L

"My friend, pay no attention to what Humbaba **promises** to you,   /L

Whatever he intends to give you now when you stand above him   /-

Will mean nothing at all the moment your body is in the dust   /-

Tablet V

Now you must not cause the thought of luxury to dissuade you." /-²⁵

Humbaba spoke to Enkidu so that his voice might be heard, /-

"You now know the character of my forest and of my environs /L

You now know all **its secrets**, but here's what I should have done /L

Apprehended and killed you as soon as you came into my forest /L

Leaving your trunk for lions to gorge upon and birds to peck at /L

Yet Enkidu, it is now within your power to save me from death /L

So will you not plea to Gilgamesh so that he might spare me?" /L

Enkidu spoke to Gilgamesh so that his voice might be heard, /L

"Friend, bring him to his final end, pulverize him, save my life /L

Be slayer of Humbaba, the demon guardian of the Pine Forest! /L

Secure your victory before supreme Ellil hears what's going on, /L

In case the gods, in retribution, unleash their fury against us: /L

Ellil in Nippur and Shamash in Sippar; but build a memorial /L

That eternally recalls the slaying of Humbaba by Gilgamesh!" /L²⁶

Humbaba heard this, **and raised his voice, speaking to Enkidu,** /L

"There you are, **holding your ground**, postured like a shepherd /L

You stand there like a servant, **waiting for your next command** /L

Yet Enkidu, it is now within your power to save me from death /L

So will you not plea to Gilgamesh so that he might spare me?" /L

Enkidu spoke to Gilgamesh so that his voice might be heard, /L

"Friend, put an end to Humbaba, who guards the Pine Forest /L

Kill him, make your death strike and pulverize him, finish him /L

Be slayer of Humbaba, the demon guardian of the Pine Forest! /L

Secure your victory before supreme Ellil hears what's going on /L

In case the gods, in retribution, unleash their fury against us: /L

Ellil in Nippur and Shamash in Sippar; but build a memorial   /L

That eternally recalls the slaying of Humbaba by Gilgamesh."   /L

Humbaba heard this **and, raising his voice, spoke to Gilgamesh,**   /L[27]

"Listen then Gilgamesh, if you wish to enjoy your prize then hear   /-

Take the Mantles of Brilliance and depart, I'll send them away   /-

And by wearing them you'll make yourself invulnerable to any."*   /-

Each of the Mantles of Brilliance flew off, one following the other   /-

Gilgamesh saw and went to chase after them, but they scattered   /-

He looked around for them, before Enkidu came and found him   /-

Enkidu raised his voice to be heard, and spoke to Gilgamesh,   /B

"Go and kill **the demon Humbaba, whom** your gods **despise?**   /B

Why do you not go to attack him but rather let him go free?"   /B

Gilgamesh raised his voice to be heard, and spoke to Enkidu,   /B

"We have to go forth now **to accomplish this task successfully**   /B

The Mantles of Brilliance are somewhere lost within the forest   /B

The Mantles of Brilliance are lost, but have also grown dim."   /B

Enkidu raised his voice to be heard, and spoke to Gilgamesh,   /B

"When you have caught a bird, friend, where are its fledglings?   /B

We can go out afterwards and seek the Mantles of Brilliance   /B

You know that like fledglings they will be out there somewhere   /B

Forget them, let us return to defeat him with his guardian **Wer.**"   /B

---

*The Sumerian version has Humbaba pass along the mantles of brilliance to Gilgamesh. It seems as though these were worn as protection by Humbaba which made him invulnerable, and when lost fled into the forest Gilgamesh sought them thinking them a peerless treasure.

Tablet V

Gilgamesh heard what he said, his mind being won over by it /B

Then the two of them shook hands; he raised the axe beside him /B

He likewise unsheathed the sword from its scabbard on his belt /B

And charged in at Humbaba and struck him right in the neck /B

Then Enkidu moved in, plunging his blade straight at his heart /B

Only one more **slash** was dealt, for then his whole body collapsed /B

All **was silent for a moment, only his whispering breath remained** /B

Humbaba raised his voice to be heard, to speak a curse to them, /-

"Neither of you two will live long, nor experience hoary old age, /L

And Gilgamesh is the one who must bury his friend, Enkidu!" /L

Enkidu spoke to Gilgamesh so that his voice might be heard, /L

"Friend, I speak words to you which you do not appear to hear, /L

Even while the curses **he flings are still echoing through the air** /L

Try now to force those curses of his back into his own mouth!" /L

Gilgamesh listened to the words that were spoken by his friend /L

Then at once pulled **from his belt the dagger** he kept at his side /L

And Gilgamesh **gave him a severe stroke, penetrating** his neck /L

Enkidu **struck him deep in the gut** until his entrails gushed out /L

From the wound of his severed head, a spring came surging up /L

Gilgamesh then collected the head, and took its teeth as a prize /L

A flood **of gory blood** cascaded down the side of the mountain /L

A rush **of red spilled** streaming down the side of the mountain /L[28]

Now the trunk of Humbaba, guardian of the Pine Forest, fell /B

Producing a boom that could be heard up to 2 leagues distant /B

Along with him **went down Wer,** then the woods' stood silently /B

He had slain **the guardian** of the Pine Forest, the woods' demon /B

Whose bellowing **had terrorized** the lands of Sirara and Lebanon /B

Whose roar was heard in the mountains, **felt upon** their heights /B

He had slain **the guardian** of the Pine Forest, the woods' demon /B

The severed **Mantles of Brilliance which had gone now** returned /B

Likewise he took nets of two talents, and arms of eight talents, /B

The total quantity of the load he took amounting to ten talents /B

Then he went out to fell the forest, within the gods' covert home /B

Enkidu and Gilgamesh then went to work in the deep forest cover /L

Gilgamesh cut down many trees, while Enkidu selected wood /L

Enkidu spoke to Gilgamesh so that his voice might be heard, /L

"My friend, I have found and downed a fully-grown pine tree /L

The crown of the tree being so lofty that it even touched the sky /L

From it I will fashion a door that is six poles high and two wide /L

Its post will be a cubit **thick**, its hinges carved from a single stem /L

It will go upon the Euphrates to Nippur, and Nippur **to Sippar,** /L

Then once in Sippar it will be taken to the temple of Shamash." /-

Then they bound together a raft, carrying it down **to the water** /L

Enkidu boarded **carrying the tree he had chosen for Shamash** /L

Gilgamesh **embarked hauling** the head of the demon Humbaba /L

(He washed the grime out of his hair, and he bathed his limbs)

TABLET VI

He washed the grime out of his hair, and he bathed his limbs   /A

Shaking out his lengthy locks so that they fell upon his back,   /A

Then he tossed his soiled clothes away and gathered clean ones   /A

Enwrapping himself in an unsullied robe and binding the sash   /A

Then Gilgamesh placed the crown of the king upon his head   /A

When Princess Ishtar saw the splendor of Gilgamesh, she said,   /A

"O Gilgamesh, make your way to me that we might make love   /A

Bequeath of your fruitfulness, we will act as husband and wife   /A

The *lapis lazuli* chariot with golden reigns will be made ready   /A

Its wheels too are made of gold, and the horns of amber-stone   /A

You'll have day-demons harnessed in place of pulling mules   /A

Gaining entry to our home you'll be overcome with pine scent   /A

Stepping upon the splendid threshold that massages your feet   /A

You will have all monarchs and nobility bowing down to you   /A

The growth of both the hills and plains will produce fruitfully   /A

You will find your goats bearing triplets, and your ewes twins   /A

Your fully stacked donkey will go more fleetly than the mule   /A

Your horses will be the most stately when drawing your chariot   /A

Your oxen will surpass any which are made to bear the yoke   /A

Gilgamesh spoke that he might be heard, to Princess Ishtar,   /A

"Truly, what is it that I could offer you if I were to have you?   /A

I could offer you oil and clothes, I could offer food and edibles   /A

But, honestly, could I give you the bread and beer of the gods?   /A

Could I provide you with a grand dwelling, make it fit for you   /-

Could I lavish **riches on you, find worthy fabric to** enrobe you?   /A

And truly, what is it that I would gain, if I were to have you?   /A

Surely you would be like a fire which is unable to melt the ice,   /A

An unsecure door which does not halt the wind and blowing,   /A

A kingdom which is **not willing to keep** its own fighting men,   /A

So too it could be of an elephant **which topples** its own shelter,   /A

So too it could be of bitumen **which marks** the one handling it,   /A

So too it could be of a water-skin **which douses** the one bearing it,   /A

So too it could be of an engine which **tumbles** a barrier of stone,   /A

So too it could be of a battering ram which topples **lofty towers**   /A

So too of a sandal which cleaves **the foot** of the one wearing it   /A

For are there any of your lovers who **have been made** immortal?   /A

Name one of your great lovers who ever joined you in heaven?   /A

Listen to me while I **describe** your many paramours with ease,   /A

Such as the shepherd, **who was far better off before** he met you;   /A

Dumuzi was your foremost lover, but he must cry now each year   /A

You were likewise so fond of the bright-feathered *allallu*-bird   /A

But when you struck him upon his wing he was sorely injured,   /A

And now he remains perched in the trees crying out 'My wing!'   /A

You even adored the regal lion, whose might is beyond compare   /A

Yet you dug seven pits—count them, seven—so as to entrap him   /A

Then you were star-struck by the horse, that dependable war pal   /A

But you made him subject to the lash, the spur, and whipping   /A

You made it so that he would have to gallop for seven leagues   /A

You made it so he would be readily fatigued and drink often /A

On top of this you cursed Sililu, his mother, with endless tears /A

You were smitten by the shepherd, the herdsman, and chief /A

Those who are forever stacking blazing embers in your name /A

And who still never fail to roast the offerings each day for you /A

But when you touched him you transformed him into a wolf, /A

Now the men who tend his own flocks seek to hunt him down /A

Now his own cherished dogs are to be found nipping at his heels /A

You were fond too of Ishullanu, who was your father's gardener /A

He carried you baskets of dates to garnish your table every day /A

You raised your eyes to flirt with him and moved closer to him, /A

'My dear Ishullanu, let me take pleasure in your perfect virility /A

Stretch out your arm, touch between my legs with your hand.' /A

Ishullanu raising his voice to be heard, spoke to Princess Ishtar, /A

'Why me, did I not have a mother who cooked that I might eat? /A

But the only bread I would receive from you would be disgrace, /A

Only marsh weeds would I have to insulate me from the cold.' /A

You listened to him, then you struck him, making him a frog /A

So that he might remain among the rushes that fed his efforts /A

But now the pole no longer rises, and the bucket no longer falls /A

And what of me, would I take you only to find myself like them?" /A

Ishtar heard this and turned livid, and travelled up into the sky /A

She went off and cried her eyes out in front of her father Anu, /A

And she also wept pathetic tears in front of her mother Antu, /A

"My father, Gilgamesh has spoken to my dishonor, repeatedly! /A

He made plain to me every disgraceful deed he could conjure /A

Speaking out loud assertions to my shame and humiliation!" /A

Anu raised his voice to be heard, and spoke to Princess Ishtar, /A

"Then why could you not confront King Gilgamesh yourself? /A

If it was Gilgamesh who conjured up these disgraceful deeds, /A

Speaking out loud assertions to your shame and humiliation?" /A

Princess Ishtar raised her voice to be heard, and spoke to Anu, /A

"Dear father, if you would but let me have the Bull of Heaven /A

Then with him I could vanquish this arrogant man Gilgamesh /A

Let me then attack Gilgamesh within his own house in Uruk /A

But here is what will ensue if you refuse me the Bull of Heaven, /A

I will smash **the gates of the Netherworld to their foundations,** /A

Then I will grant emancipation to the underworld dominions, /A

And thus will cause the dead to arise, and consume the living /A

Thereby I will make it so the dead outnumber those that live!" /A

Then Anu raised his voice to be heard, and spoke to Ishtar, /A

"Only under these terms might you have the Bull of Heaven: /A

The widow of Uruk must collect seven years' worth of leavings, /A

And the farmer of Uruk must grow seven years' worth of hay." /A

Princess Ishtar raised her voice to be heard, speaking to Anu, /A

"I have stored up monumental stocks of seed within Uruk /A

And made certain there would grow **an abundance of grain** /A

The widow of Uruk has collected seven years' worth of leavings, /A

And the farmer **of Uruk** has grown seven years' worth of hay /A

Give me the leash of the Bull of Heaven, **I will set things right!"** /A

Tablet VI

Anu heard everything which Ishtar had been speaking,   /A
And he put the leash of the Bull of Heaven within her hand   /A
Then Ishtar led forth the bull and descended down with it   /A
When it had reached the lands around the city of Uruk,   /A
It dehydrated the forest; the marshes and reed-beds dried,   /A
Then it descended to the river, reducing it by seven cubits   /A
And when the Bull of Heaven snorted once, a rift opened   /A
One-hundred of the young men of Uruk were lost into it   /A
Then two-hundred young men, three-hundred young men   /A
When it snorted a second time another rift was opened,   /A
And yet again a hundred young men of Uruk were lost   /A
Then two-hundred young men, three-hundred young men   /A
Then when it snorted a third time yet another rift opened,   /A
This time Enkidu was partly swallowed, but leapt out again,   /A
And he took the Bull of Heaven, grasping it by the horns   /A
The Bull of Heaven spat at his face, swinging its hefty tail   /A

Enkidu spoke to Gilgamesh, so his voice would be heard,   /A
"Brother, we spoke fulsomely among the people of our city   /A
So mustn't we live up to our words to them with actions?   /A
Friend, I have gauged the strength of the Bull **of Heaven**   /A
And thus knowing how strong it is, **and what it might do**   /A
Now I will **judge** for a second time the strength of this bull,   /A
By putting **myself at the** hindquarters **of the Bull of Heaven,**   /A
And I will grab the bull, taking it by the tuft of its hefty tail   /A

67

Then I will **set** my foot, securing it against **the back of its** leg /A

In **doing this you will be able to leap onto the beast's back** /A

Then you will drive your sword, being brave and precise, /A

Right between its horn-base and the tendons of its neck." /A

So Enkidu went around to the hindquarters of the Bull, /A

And grabbed the beast, taking it by the tuft of its hefty tail /A

Then set his foot, secured against **the back of the Bull's** leg /A

In **doing this he was able to leap up onto the beast's back,** /A

Then Gilgamesh drove his sword, being brave and precise, /A

Right between its horn-base and the tendons of its neck /A

Now having slain the Bull, they offered its heart to Shamash, /A

Moving a respectable distance they bowed before Shamash /A

Then each of the brothers found a place to seat himself /A

But Ishtar appeared on the wall of Uruk, the Sheep Pen, /A

Blazing with anger, launching a hail of curses upon them /A

"Gilgamesh, who spurned me, killed the Bull of Heaven!" /A

Enkidu had listened to what Ishtar had been speaking, /A

And tore the shoulder of the Bull of Heaven from its socket /A

Wielding it with disdain he threw it so that it struck her face /A

"If only I were able to reach you there as that shoulder did, /A

For I would strike you in the face myself if I were able to, /A

Taking its sordid intestines, draping them on your arms!" [*] /A

---

[*] As in the prior circumstance in Tablet 4, in the Sumerian version the text runs:

An axe of 7 talents, **wielded by Gilgamesh,** crashed into its skull

Raising its head one last time, before the bull fell from its height

Tablet VI

Ishtar then called together the many women of ill repute, /A

And set forth the mourning over the Bull of Heaven's leg /A

Gilgamesh summoned men who work metal and cast armor /A

These skilled men looked with wonder at the girth of its horns /A

They determined thirty *minas* of *lapis lazuli* for each open end /A

They determined two *minas* of gold for each of their casings /A

They found that each within its volume held a full six vats of oil /A

He dedicated these to the anointing of his divinity Lugalbanda[*] /A

As family head, he lifted them up and hung them from his bed /A

They went to wash their hands in the water of the Euphrates /A

They took hands and then rode down the boulevard of Uruk /A

There the people of the city had assembled to catch a glimpse /A

Then Gilgamesh asked a question of his many fine noblemen, /A

"Who is the best among the youth, and highest among men?" /A

(And the noblemen raised their voices in reply, to Gilgamesh,)

"Gilgamesh is best among the youth, and highest among men! /A

Of this we always were aware, even when we had been enraged /A

No other could hope to please her, satisfy **the daughter-in-law.**" /A

Then they took hands and together they entered into the palace /-

Gilgamesh enjoined and enjoyed the festivity within his home /A

Taking the formless shape of a clay pile, *lying flat like cut barley*

With no butcher around, the king took a knife in his own hand,

And cut off one of its thighs, which he threw straight at Inanna

She took to the air like a dove, and instead he destroyed the wall

[*] The mortal father of Gilgamesh

Then settled down to sleep, the young men slept for the night   /A

Enkidu lay down with the rest of them, and slept and dreamed   /A

When he awoke he recalled the dream, speaking to his friend,   /A

(When the dawn broke, Enkidu rose and spoke to Gilgamesh)

TABLET VII

When the dawn broke, Enkidu rose and spoke to Gilgamesh,   /H[29]

"My friend, did I have a dream to speak of during the night!   /H

But why would I have seen the great gods consulting together?   /A

Anu, Ellil, and Ea, along with the holy Shamash were gathered   /H

Then Anu raised his voice foremost and, speaking to Ellil, said,   /H

'Now that these two warriors have destroyed the Bull of Heaven   /H

Just as they killed Humbaba, the guardian of the Pine Forest,   /H

Surely now we must admit that one of them is soon fated to die.'   /H

Then Ellil raised his voice to be heard, speaking in reply to Anu, /H

'If one must die let it be Enkidu, so that Gilgamesh might live.'   /H

Then holy Shamash, raised his voice to be heard, saying to Ellil, /H

'Was it not because of you that they killed the Bull of Heaven,   /H

So too Humbaba; now should blameless Enkidu be doomed?'   /H

Ellil was irate at this and, turning to holy Shamash, said to him, /H

'It was you who travelled with them each day, like a companion.'" /H

Enkidu then sat down in front of Gilgamesh, his tears gushing,   /H

"You are loved, my brother, yet they take me from my friend   /H

I will take my seat among the dead, **set within** the mausoleum, /H

No longer will I be able to set my eyes upon my dear brother."   /H

Enkidu raised his voice to be heard, and spoke to Gilgamesh,   /A

"Then let us go **together, my brother, and seek a remedy for this,** /A

There **set within the temple of Shamash is an object to consult,** /A

The door **which we brought from the Pine Forest, made of wood,**   /A

Since **it has a unique quality, and it possesses a singular nature,**   /A

Surely such a thing has some sort of debt to us for what we did   /-

Surely if we have done good for it, it will do us a favor in return   /-

Let us traverse our way to the temple of Shamash, and ask of it."   /-

Enkidu raised **himself off the floor and they went to the temple**   /A

He spoke of **the matter of the dream standing** before the door,   /A

"O door, are you capable of conscious thought, or are you not?   /A

I chose the wood of which you were made out of twenty leagues,   /A

Before I located an ancient pine, so no timber is similar to you,   /A

You were made to be in size six poles high and two poles wide,   /A

Your post, as well as your hinges, were carved from a lone tree   /A

You went upon the Euphrates to Nippur, **and Nippur to Sippar**   /A

Realize then, door, that this was something good **we did** for you,   /A

This was an honor which you received from us, **which we did**   /A

It was I who lifted the axe which struck you, causing you to fall,   /A

It was I who loaded you upon the raft which came to Ebabbara   /A

To bring you all the way here to Ebabbara, to Shamash's temple   /A

It was I who installed you at the gate **of entry into** his holy shrine   /A

And in it placed illustrations of the Anzu-bird and Great Bull   /A

Also having given your passageway precedence over all others,   /A

As I brought you to the city of Uruk, to the temple of Shamash,   /A

Here in Uruk **you are recognized by many, your wood admired,**   /A

All because Shamash had heard my plea when I spoke to him,   /A

When facing danger, he remembered me and came with arms   /A

So realize, door, it was I who created you, brought you to Nippur,   /A

But just as surely could I rip you out and then smash you to bits /A

For the master who comes after me will use you to go in and out, /A

Or **rather someone will** relocate you to a different spot altogether /A

And he will deface my own name and inscribe there his own!" /A

With that he tore **the door from its hinges**, tossing **it in the street** /A

And he was listening to his words and suddenly started crying, /A

Gilgamesh heard what his friend Enkidu said, and began to cry /A

So Gilgamesh raised his voice, and spoke to **his brother** Enkidu, /A

"My friend, **before I considered your reasoning to be** unequalled /A

I used to find that your speech made sense, but what of it now! /A

My brother, why does your inner voice speak in such a manner /A

Your dream was singular, the portent dire, your grief quite plain, /A

The portent was dire, your dream was singular, your grief plain, /A

It was clear that the gods will bring heart-strain to the survivor /A

Your dream indicates heart-strain for the one who will survive /A

So then I will make my way to the high gods and entreat them, /A

Go to **whichever goddess guards you,** and seek your patron god, /A

Anu, ruler and father of the gods, Ellil the supreme authority, /A

To them will I address my prayers; **and may Ea be attendant** /A

A statue will be made of you, with innumerable gold **fittings** /A

There is no reason for you to contribute silver, gold, or **gems** /A

For the word of Ellil is not the same as **that of the other** gods, /A

His words are not like **the wind**, he doesn't ever retract them, /A

The words he speaks **aren't worthless,** and aren't wiped out." /A

(Enkidu raised his voice to be heard, speaking to Gilgamesh)

"My friend, nothing can be done; people die before their time."   /A

When dawn broke, Enkidu **looked up**, crying out to Shamash,   /A
His tears rained down before the streaming beams of sunlight,   /A
"I plead with you, Shamash, because I was not fated the same   /A
The hunter, the trapper, caused me to gain less than my friend   /A
So let the hunter himself not gain as much as his friend gains   /A
Strip away his pre-eminence, cause him to be far less successful   /A
Make his portion be far diminished when you determine his fate   /A
Let **good fortune** remain outside, cause it to flee out his window!"   /A
Then after he had condemned the hunter to his heart's content,   /A
He also brought condemnation upon Shamhat, the prostitute,   /A
"Now you enter, Shamhat, and I will set your destiny as well,   /A
And let it be your fate without end, and be yours for all time   /A
Thus will I condemn you with the most obnoxious of curses,   /A
Forthwith, you will feel the force of my condemnations strike!   /A
You will find that your house will forsake its seductive appeal   /A
You will not give rise to a family and be mother to proud sons,   /A
You will not see them enter into the rooms of unmarried girls   /A
Your covetous lap will be covered only with the foulest rubbish,   /A
And your bright garment tainted by the vomit of the drunken   /A
Only tarnished copper will you ever have to decorate your finger   /A
You'll find your face cream in the potter's discarded clay heap,   /A
You'll be prevented from acquiring the best **powder for your face**   /A
No shining silver, the gain of wealth, will be found upon you,   /A

The **habitation for you** your **whole life** will be the front porch,   /A

The traveler's crossroads will be the only place to seat yourself,   /A

The empty lots will be the only location where you can rest,   /A

Under the shadows of the city wall the only place you can lie,   /A

You will find thorns and nails puncturing the soles of your feet   /A

You will find the drunk and the covetous striking your cheek,   /A

You will find the worthy crowd casting accusations your way,   /A

You will not find the builder come to seal **the leak in your roof**,   /A

And you will have night birds building nests **in your rafters**   /A

There will not be a time when feasts will be enjoyed with you,   /A

And not come a time when the instruments are played for you   /-

You will not get to enjoy the company of fine folks for very long,   /-

You will spend your youth soliciting and your old age begging   /-

This is the kind of life you have been cursed to live, by my words   /-

Reason being that you corrupted me when 1 knew not better,   /A

Because you seduced me in the wilderness in my innocence!"   /A

Shamash listened to every word that Enkidu had been speaking,   /A

Just then a booming voice came to him from out of the clouds,   /A

"Enkidu, for what reason do you condemn Shamhat, my harlot?   /A

Was it not she who fed you upon food suitable only for gods   /A

Was it not she who gave you beer suitable only for the mighty   /A

Was it not she who gathered and set superb raiment upon you,   /A

And brought you to Gilgamesh, the best friend you ever had?   /A

But Gilgamesh, who is not just a friend to you but a brother,   /A

He will set you down to lie stricken upon an exceptional bed   /A

And will set you down to recline upon a pillow of tenderness,   /A

So that you will remain in the peaceful place, situated to the left   /A

Then you will find the rulers of earth coming to kiss your feet,   /A

He will cause Uruk's people to mourn you with tearful weeping,   /A

He will cause a deep affliction to pervade a formidable people   /A

Then he will even fail to care for his own self after you are gone   /A

Wrapping himself in only a lion skin, wandering the wilderness."   /A

Enkidu listened to every word spoken by the warrior Shamash   /A

And then his fury left him, his emotions were stilled within him,   /A

Having been given to anger, his emotions were quelled in him,   /A

"Now you enter again, Shamhat, and I will alter your destiny!   /A

What I said before to condemn will now be utterances of praise   /A

Rulers and princes will share their deepest fondness with you,   /A

The man at one-league will be known to strike his thigh for you   /A

The man at two-leagues will be known to let go his hair for you   /A

Even the herdsman will not refrain, who releases his belt for you   /A

You shall receive from him the best ivory, gold, and *lapis lazuli*   /A

And the finest rings and clasps will be the gifts you shall receive   /A

Ishtar, the most charming of the gods, will give you easy ingress   /A

Into the home of the family man, whose storeroom jars are full   /A

For your sake the honest mother, who gave birth, will be alone."   /A

Following this Enkidu **cried,** for he was pained deeply by it all,   /A

Then he went inside of the house and took his place to lie down   /A

And spoke of what he was thinking of so his friend might know,   /A

"Hear me speak again, my brother, of a dream I had last night   /A

When heaven spoke loudly and the earth reverberated in reply,   /A

And there I was standing with these two upon either side of me   /A

Also there was a young man there, but whose face was ominous,   /A

And he had a face which resembled that of the great Anzu-bird   /A

But his hands were like a lion's paws, armed with eagles' talons   /A

With overwhelming force, he grabbed hold of me by my hair   /A

So I struck him smartly, and he leapt as a springing-toy does,   /A

He struck me once and I was tossed over like an upset canoe   /A

And he treaded upon me as though he were a stomping buffalo   /A

Until my body was crushed, and wet from its venomous slobber   /A

And I cried, 'Help me, my brother, come to my aid, leave me not!'   /A

Yet you were so fearful that you did nothing **to come to my aid,**   /A

You **stood there rigid like a stone, without your knees shifting,**   /A

Though you looked as though you were ready to come to my aid   /-

Though you carried your weapons and were clad in your armor,   /-

You stood there rigid like a stone, without your knees shifting   /-

Then he struck me again and I was transformed into a dove,   /A

Binding my limbs, in the same manner in which a foul is tied   /A

Then took me and led me into the dark realm of Erkalla's god   /A

The dwelling which once one has entered he can never depart   /A

Whereupon the road travelled can only be traversed one way   /A

Within the house whose guests will see nothing more of light   /A

There only dust is given as food, and only clay is given as bread,   /A

Where their bodies are covered with feathers, like those of foul* /A

There no illumination is to be seen, they exist only in darkness /A

Where upon the door top and upon the lock, dust has gathered /A

I gazed at the walls around me, and there was a pile of crowns /A

Surely these belonged to crowned heads who ruled in ages past, /A

The priests of Anu and Ellil at regular times set out roasted meat, /A

They placed out baked bread, poured out water from water-skins /A

There within that dwelling of the ground that I had come upon, /A

There lived the high and elder, the prophetic, and spirit-priests, /A

Also the unshorn priests of the high gods, Etana, and Shakkan,† /A

There lived Ereshkigal, Queen of the Earth and the Underworld /A

Also there was Belet-seri, the earth's scribe, seated before her /A

She held in her hand a tablet and was reading aloud from it /A

Then lifted her eyes and took me in, asking, 'Who invited him?'" /A[30]

Gilgamesh listened as Enkidu finished telling his dream to him, /-

Enkidu looked progressively pale as he spoke, his life ebbed, /-

Then Gilgamesh raised his voice to him, speaking to his brother, /-

"We have contested before and you were the one who prevailed, /-

Together we were able to overcome Humbaba of the Pine Forest /(A)

Together we killed lions that lived in the dark mountain passes, /(A)

And took the Bull of Heaven, flinging him down from the sky, /(A)

Together we have faced and overcome all manner of adversaries /A

Do not forget about me, my brother, and of what we have done /A

---

* Those in the Underworld were thought to have wings and feathers.

† Respectively, the king of Kish and the god of cattle

Tablet VII

My brother witnessed a dream which was beyond utterance /A

And from that day forward he began to lose his formidability." /A

So then Enkidu remained lying there for one day and then two /A

Resting upon the mat, Enkidu's malady grew, his body failed /A

The third and fourth, Enkidu's malady grew, his body failed /A

The fifth, sixth, and seventh; the eighth, ninth, and tenth day, /A

Enkidu's malady became greater and his body became weaker /A

The eleventh and twelfth, the malady worsened, his body failed /A

Enkidu was lying upon his mat **motionless, and he did not stir** /A

And Gilgamesh called out to him, **he spoke but received no reply,** /A

"My friend blames me **for what happened to us in our dire peril,** /A

Because when we were in the midst of **the passes the lions came** /A

Yet I was far too fearful to attack, **and would not raise my blade** /A

And my friend, **who engaged willfully** in the battle, **he reviled me,** /A

And I, in **fear, did not act to obliterate the curse he set upon me."** /A[31]

Then Enkidu let loose a cry, **and Gilgamesh was shaken by it,** /B

And his spirit issued forth from his lips in a form like a dove, /B

His body then became motionless, and the sky became **dark,** /B

And Gilgamesh stayed with him all during the hours of night /B

Then the greatest of **all men, Enkidu's best friend, Gilgamesh,** /B

Pledged what he would undertake for the sake of his brother, /B

"I will cry **for my friend, to mourn with grief like a wailing wife** /B

So now regarding **this axe** beside me, **and my forearm spike,** /B

The sword in its sheath, and the shield held rigid before me, /(A)

My ostentatious clothing, and my broad commanding sash,   /(A)

Cruel fortune did emerge and stole them from my possession   /(A)

My friend was a mule pursued, a feral ass, a leopard of the plains   /(A)

The burly man, Enkidu, was a mule pursued, and was a feral ass,   /(A)

He was a leopard of the plains, and we who became companions,   /(A)

Together we climbed the foothills up into the precipitous country,   /(A)

We took hold of the Bull of Heaven and brought about its demise   /(A)

We destroyed Humbaba, the terrible guardian of the Pine Forest   /(A)

But what now is this quiescence which has taken hold of you?   /(A)

Now you are no longer awake, and do not pay attention to me?   /(A)

He is not able to raise up his head, he is not able to move his lips   /(A)

And when I place my hand upon his chest, I feel no heartbeat."   /(A)

(When the dawn rays shone, Gilgamesh spoke to his companion)

TABLET VIII

When the dawn rays shone, Gilgamesh spoke to his companion,   /A

"My brother Enkidu, you were born from a gazelle of a mother   /A

And sired by a father who was a feral donkey rather than a man,   /A

They tasted the milk of the wild ass, the parents who reared you   /A

And the wild cattle familiarized you with the best grazing land   /A

And Enkidu's walking ways took him into the vast Pine Forest   /A

You'll find them weeping for you day and night, never ceasing,   /A

The elders of the vast city, Uruk the Sheep Pen, will weep for you   /A

The people who gave us their heartfelt wishes, will weep for you   /A

The highest peak will honor us after we are gone, you and me   /A

The **animals** of the mountains will shed abundant tears for you   /A

The beasts of the grasslands will be in heavy mourning for you   /A

The wilderness will cry like a father, the meadow like a mother,   /A

Likewise shall it be with the pine, the myrtle, and the cypress,   /A

Which surrounded us when we took our weapons with fervor   /A

So too will cry the bears, hyenas, leopards, tigers, and horses,   /A

The cheetah, lions, buffalo, deer, mountain goats, and aurochs,   /A

Likewise the other wild animals which inhabit the countryside   /A

Ulaya, the river beside which we walked in confidence, will weep   /A

The clear Euphrates, which provided water for our water-skins,   /A

Whose cool waters gave tender for our thirst, will weep for you   /A

The young men of the wide city, Uruk the Sheep Pen, will weep   /A

Who saw the contest when together we faced the Bull of Heaven   /A

And the man who walks behind the steer too shall weep for you   /A

The one who praises your name with the favorable sound 'alala'   /A

The priests of the wide city, Uruk the Sheep Pen, will weep also   /A

Those who will raise praise to your name in the very first **descant**   /A

Both the shepherd and herdsman, by and by, will weep for you,   /A

Who provided sweet butter and milk that touched your tongue   /A

And **the nurse** who once applied the salve to your limbs will weep   /A

The medicine man who gave you distillations to drink shall weep,   /A

The one who produced the brew for the ale that lapped your lips   /A

The prostitute, who anointed you with perfume, will weep for you   /A

The mother-in-law and father-in-law shall likewise weep for you   /A

Who **are caretakers of** the bride, the one **who magnifies** your loins   /A

Along with the young men, who are your kin forever, will weep   /A

Their hair will fall loosely upon their backs, like the womenfolk   /A

They will cry out your name, and grab their hair because of you   /A

As will I, who am like both a mother and father to you, Enkidu,   /A

Shed an abundance of tears on your former tramping ground   /A

Heed me, young men of Uruk, and listen to what I have to say!   /A

Heed me, elders of vast Uruk, and listen to what I have to say!   /A

I must cry for my brother, to mourn with grief like a wailing wife   /A

So now regarding this axe beside me, and my forearm spike,   /A

The sword in its sheath, and the shield held rigid before me,   /A

My ostentatious clothing, and my broad commanding sash,   /A

Cruel **fortune** did emerge and stole them from my possession   /A

My friend was a mule pursued, a feral ass, a leopard of the plains   /A

.

The burly man, Enkidu, was a mule pursued, and was a feral ass,   /A

He was a leopard of the plains, and we who became companions,   /A

Together we climbed the foothills up into the precipitous country,   /A

We took hold of the Bull of Heaven and brought about its demise   /A

We destroyed Humbaba, the terrible guardian of the Pine Forest   /A

But what now is this quiescence which has taken hold of you?   /A

Now you are no longer awake, and do not pay attention to me?   /A

He is not able to raise up his head, he is not able to move his lips   /A

And when I place my hand upon his chest, I feel no heartbeat."   /A

Then, like the bride with a veil, he enshrouded his friend's face   /A

He hovered above him, encircling like an eagle searching for prey   /A

As does a lioness likewise when her cubs have fallen into a trap   /A

So he walked, strode without purpose, pacing this way and that,   /A

He grabbed and mussed the splendidly curling locks of his hair,   /A

Tore off and discarded his royal finery like something degraded   /A

When the dawn shone, Gilgamesh proclaimed across the land   /A

To the smith, **goldsmith**, coppersmith, silversmith, and jeweler,   /A

To have a statue prepared, **made in the likeness** of his dear friend   /A

And his four limbs were formed **of metal**, his torso of *lapis lazuli,*   /A

His flesh was fashioned out of gold, **his hair was cast in bronze,**   /A[32]

His body was made whole through the use of bellows and tongs,   /-

His flesh was hammered into place and burnished until it shone   /-

His coat was covered with splendid gems, his eyes were sapphires   /-

He was draped in his royal clothes, graced by his fearsome arms   /-

His sword belt clasped, his axes grasped in hands of white ivory   /-

His dagger was set within its scabbard, his armor upon his chest   /-

But Gilgamesh would not let them bury him, but kept at his side   /-

Upon him he cried for six days and as many intervening nights   /(A)

But would not let them bury him 'til a worm fell from his nose   /(A)

He was so scared and fearful to think that he had been overcome   /(A)

Then when it was finished Gilgamesh spoke to Enkidu, saying,   /-

"Now I will set you to recline forever upon a pillow of tenderness,   /A

So that you will remain in this peaceful place, situated to the left   /A

And you will find the rulers of earth will come to kiss your feet,   /A

I will cause Uruk's people to mourn you with tearful weeping,   /A

And I will cause a deep affliction to pervade a formidable people   /A

Then I will even fail to care for my own self after you are gone   /A

And will wear only a lion skin, wandering the empty wilderness."   /A

When the dawn shone, Gilgamesh arose and entered the treasury   /A

Opening the lock, pulling aside the bolt, gazing upon the riches   /A

From amongst it he chose blocks of *carnelian*, marble, *gypsum*   /A

Placing the pieces he took over in a pile which he slowly built up   /A

Those which he selected as an offering to the gods for his brother   /A[33]

All manner of treasures were brought forth, expertly crafted   /A

An extensive hoard of brass vessels he presented to his friend   /A

An extensive hoard of silver vessels he presented to his friend   /A

An extensive hoard of gold treasures he presented to his friend   /-[34]

A large elaborate shield that he bore he presented to his friend   /A

A decorated dagger from at his waist he presented to his friend   /A

A perfectly wrought golden helmet he presented to his friend /A

Complete hammered bronze armor he presented to his friend /A

A leather coat with studded bronze he presented to his friend /A

The greaves which protected his legs he presented to his friend /A

The guards which covered his feet he presented to his friend /A

A Damascus sword made with an ivory pommel of one talent, /A

With a gold hilt made of six minas, he presented to his friend /A

A strong bow, of three cubit length, he presented to his friend /A

And a bow with a quiver of decorated lapis lazuli, horn tipped, /A

Set with a gold handle, of one talent, he presented to his friend /A

And a composite bow, the ends of its length tipped with ivory, /A

Set with a gold handle of 40 minas, he presented to his friend /A

A bow made entirely of bone, which was three cubits in length, /A

With gold tips, and one pole thick, he presented to his friend /A

A cart of fine gold, with inlays of *carnelian*, and axle of iron /A

Pulled and led with a rope which ran to the leader of the ox /A

Both the cart and everything within he presented to his friend /A

Then animals were sacrificed; oxen and rams were heaped up /A

These were shown to Shamash before being set within the tomb /A

They were dispatched to give nourishment for the Earth gods /A

The first offering to be given to the gods was for Princess Ishtar /A

A rod of fine cedar wood given to Ishtar, Queen of the Heavens /A

This was shown to Shamash before being set within the tomb /A

(Gilgamesh raised his voice to be heard, addressing the deity,)

"May Ishtar, Queen of the Heavens, receive this gift with favor, /A

That she greet Enkidu, guide him on his way, and be his escort /A

(Treat him as your cherished guest, that he not be distressed.")

A box of fine olive wood given for Namrasit, **lord of the moon** /A

This was shown to Shamash before being set within the tomb /A

(Gilgamesh raised his voice to be heard, addressing this deity,) /A

"May Namrasit, **lord of the moon,** receive this gift with favor, /A

That he greet Enkidu, guide him on his way, and be his escort /A

(Treat him as your cherished guest, that he not be distressed.")

An ointment jar of *lapis lazuli* **was given with especial meaning** /A

He provided this jar for Ereshkigal, Queen of the Netherworld /A

This was shown to Shamash before being set within the tomb /A

(Gilgamesh raised his voice to be heard, addressing the deity,)

"May Ereshkigal, Queen of the Netherworld, accept this gift, /A

That she greet Enkidu, guide him on his way, and be his escort /A

(Treat him as your cherished guest, that he not be distressed.")

He brought forth a whistle made of _carnelian_, crafted with care, /-

He provided this for the shepherd Dumuzi, whom Ishtar loved, /A

This was shown to Shamash before being set within the tomb /A

(Gilgamesh raised his voice to be heard, addressing the deity,)

"May Dumuzi, shepherd whom Ishtar loved, accept this gift, /A

That he greet Enkidu, guide him on his way, and be his escort /A

(Treat him as your cherished guest, that he not be distressed.")

A precious throne **and matching** staff fully made of *lapis lazuli* /A

Namtar, who was chief official of the Earth, was given this gift /A

These were shown to Shamash before being set within the tomb   /A

(Gilgamesh raised his voice to be heard, addressing the deity,)

"May Namtar, who is chief official of the Earth, accept this gift,   /A

That he greet Enkidu, guide him on his way, and be his escort   /A

(Treat him as your cherished guest, that he not be distressed.")

A brilliant gemmed necklace was produced for Namtar's spouse   /-

He provided this for Hushbisha, matron of the Netherworld,   /A

This was shown to Shamash before being set within the tomb   /A

(Gilgamesh raised his voice to be heard, addressing the deity,)

"May Hushbisha, matron of the Netherworld, accept this gift,   /A

That she greet Enkidu, guide him on his way, and be his escort   /A

(Treat him as your cherished guest, that he not be distressed.")

Next he had made a fine bracelet of **rubies**, mounted in silver,   /A

He provided this for Qassu-tabat, who cleaned for Ereshkigal,   /A

This was shown to Shamash before being set within the tomb   /A

"May Qassu-tabat, the cleaner for Ereshkigal, accept this gift,   /A

That she greet Enkidu, guide him on his way, and be his escort   /A

Treat him as your cherished guest, that he not be distressed."   /A

There was a decorated broach which depicted the Pine Forest   /A

Made of marble, inlaid with stones of *lapis lazuli* and *carnelian*   /A

This was given for Ninshuluhha, the housekeeper of Ereshkigal   /A

This was shown to Shamash before being set within the tomb   /A

"May Ninshuluhha, Ereshkigal's housekeeper, accept this gift,   /A

That she greet Enkidu, guide him on his way, and be his escort   /A

And might she brighten the surroundings in front of my friend   /A

Treat him as your cherished guest, that he not be distressed." /A

An exquisite double-bladed saber, with a *lapis lazuli* pommel /A

And upon it was carved the curving flow of the clear Euphrates /A

It was to be given to Bibbu, who was the Netherworld's butcher /A

This was shown to Shamash before being set within the tomb /A

"May Bibbu, the butcher of the Netherworld, accept this gift, /A

That he greet Enkidu, guide him on his way, and be his escort /A

(Treat him as your cherished guest, that he not be distressed.")

He took an ebony stool with a leather seat and back of *gypsum* /A

This was for Dumuzi-abzu, the Netherworld's sacrificial priest, /A

This was shown to Shamash before being set within the tomb /A

"May Dumuzi-abzu, the Netherworld's priest, accept this gift, /A

That he greet Enkidu, guide him on his way, and be his escort /A

(Treat him as your cherished guest, that he not be distressed.")

To this he added a splendid table with a cover of *lapis lazuli* /A

Both its base and legs were made of ebony, inlaid with *carnelian* /A

This was a present for Nedu, the head gatekeeper of the Earth /-

This was shown to Shamash before being set within the tomb /(A)

"May Nedu, the head gatekeeper of the Earth, accept this gift, /-

That he greet Enkidu, guide him on his way, and be his escort /(A)

(Treat him as your cherished guest, that he not be distressed,")

Then Gilgamesh raised his voice to be heard, speaking to Enkidu, /(A)

"O my friend who I loved so, and who met every peril with me, /(A)

O Enkidu who I loved so, and who met every peril at my side, /(A)

The destiny which awaits all mortals did likewise conquer him /(A)

The friend who I loved so, he will be reduced to dust and clay /(A)

Enkidu, the one I loved so, he will be reduced to dust and clay /(A)

And is my life not the same, that I must lie never again to rise?" /(A)

When this had been completed the high priests spoke the eulogy, /-³⁵

"May the gods, as we have, recognize the greatness they shared /A

So that the gods of heaven will forget not their names and deeds /A

Preserve Gilgamesh to be high king and the Anunnaki's judge." /A

When Gilgamesh had heard this, he thought to better the way /A

When the dawn rays shone, Gilgamesh threw the doors wide /A

There was placed out in the open a large table of Syrian wood, /A

Honey was put in a *carnelian* bowl, butter in one of *lapis lazuli* /A

Everything was properly prepared and shown before Shamash /A

All these offerings were poured out, for the god's good favor³⁶ /A

(Gilgamesh was overcome and mourned over his friend Enkidu)

TABLET IX

Gilgamesh was overcome and mourned over his friend Enkidu, /A

And so he wore only a lion-skin, and wandered the wilderness, /A

"Is death my fate too, for is my life not the same as Enkidu's? /A

Beset by an overwhelming anguish that has penetrated my core, /A

So fearful am I of impending death that I wander the wilderness /A

I must travel as fast as I can, to Utnapishtim, son of Ubara-Tutu /A

At night in the mountain passes, lions that came frightened me /A

So I lifted up my eyes and made a prayer to Sin, heaven's **lantern** /A

'Oh great lord Sin, as you look upon me now, preserve me now!' /A

Enkidu, who had gone to sleep, was startled out of his dream[*] /A

When he leapt up he was greatly possessed of a fervent instinct /A

And he grasped the axe beside him, and unsheathed his sword /A

As fast as a dart he quickly leapt among them and took them on /A

There he gave blows **with his weapons**, and smashed **their skulls** /A

The following day **he went out, standing before Shamash** at noon /A

And he gave **the bodies of the lions to him as a thank offering** /A

He carved **out their hearts, offering them to the spirits by name**[†] /A[37]

Then he spoke to Shamash, giving him thanks for his aid, saying, /-

'O Shamash, every day you are the one who rules over the world /-

When you arise, your fire extinguishes the other fires of heaven /-

---

[*] This episode could also be about Gilgamesh, and occurring at this time rather than as a recollection.

[†] It is particularly uncertain as to what occurred at this point; the original fragmentary lines read: "He then carved...The first being named...The second being named...".

And the entirety of humanity calls out in praise to you, Shamash,   /-
The world which desires your illumination calls for your coming,   /-
Man prays aloft to you, his voice is nothing more than a whisper   /-
He calls upon you when his kin are nowhere near, his dwelling far   /-
O mighty Shamash, through the strength you gave me did we live   /-
Now are these dedicated to you for bringing us into your service   /-
May your light never be shed from our heads, and preserve us.'"   /-
And Gilgamesh turned his face to his shield, the warrior Shamash   /-
Shamash watched and considered, speaking to himself, saying,   /(A)
"You have made your way through a great many hard countries   /(A)
And have traversed your way over and across every body of water   /(A)
And you hunt the bear, hyena, lion, leopards, tigers, and deer   /(A)
Mountain goats, buffalo, and other wild animals of the country   /(A)
And you consume their meat, and clothe yourself in their hides   /B
But you attempt to seize the ripples spread across **the Euphrates**   /B
They are not real, Gilgamesh, only wind running over the waters."   /B
And Shamash was troubled, and lowered to speak to Gilgamesh,   /B
"Gilgamesh, what is your destination as you search aimlessly   /B
No matter how far you roam, you'll not find your eternal youth."   /B
Gilgamesh raised his voice, speaking to the warrior Shamash,   /B
"As long as I am roaming across the countryside, I am yet alive!   /B
There is plenty of sleep for those who reside in the Underworld   /B
Would I rather spend my years on earth getting even more sleep?   /B
Rather I would let my eyes gaze upon the sun, and be given light,   /B
There is nothing to be had in darkness, but how precious light is!   /B

Once the man is dead will he look upon the sun's beams again?"   /B

Shamash listened to everything Gilgamesh had spoken, and said,   /-

"By what you've said you prevail upon me to act as your guide,   /-

And I will set you upon your way, despite that it remains fruitless,   /-

Make your way east to mountains which are called the Mashu."   /A

So Gilgamesh continued onward until he arrived at one Mashu[*]   /A

Which is the guardian of Shamash when he rises each morning,   /A

Their high peaks reach up to the very underpinnings of the sky   /A

In the other direction their bases extend down to deep Arallu[†]   /A

And there guarding the gate were the legions of scorpion-men   /A

Their very form strikes one with terror, having the look of death   /A

It is their Mantles of Brilliance which enshrouded the mountains   /A

It is they who are guardians of the sun both at sunrise and sunset   /A

Gilgamesh gazed at them, his face overcome by a fear and dread   /A

But he made his first move, approaching them in the usual way   /A

The scorpion-man then called out, alerting his wife of his coming,   /A

"There is a man here to see us who is made of the flesh of gods."   /A

The scorpion-man's wife called back, and answered him, saying,   /A

"Only two-thirds he is a god, the other third of him is yet mortal."   /A

Then the male scorpion-man called to the god-man Gilgamesh,   /A

"Does this not look like a man who long ago set out on his quest,   /A

Who comes into my presence, **who makes** this difficult passage?   /A

---

[*] There are two Mashu mountains, one at the point of sunrise and one at the point of sunset.

[†] The Underworld

92

First of all, *tell me your* **name and the place of your family tomb** /A

Second of all, *tell me* **what people you are from, what city you flee."** /A[38]

Gilgamesh raising his voice to be heard, said to the scorpion-man, /(A)

"Look at me again, and gaze upon this sore-stricken face of mine /(A)

Know then that I have become a companion of the wilderness /(A)

You must have heard of me, I am the King of Uruk, Gilgamesh, /(A)

And I am on a journey to seek out Utnapishtim, the faraway, /(A)

He whom the people spoke of, so I sought through every land /(A)

I made my way into and through a great many hard countries /(A)

And have traversed my way over and across every body of water /(A)

Never was I able to get enough sleep, I was so sorely beset inside /(A)

And from this deficiency of sleep did I become even more restless /(A)

But I have now to ask myself what good it does me to suffer so? /(A)

I have hunted the bear, hyena, lion, leopards, tigers, and deer /(A)

Mountain goats, buffalo, and other wild animals of the country /(A)

And I consumed their meat, and clothed myself in their hides /(A)

It is from my own bad fortunes that I have been driven to despair." /(A)

Gilgamesh raising his voice to be heard, said to the scorpion-man, /(A)

"Concerning Utnapishtim, *the faraway, my father* **spoke of him** /A

Who stood within the gods' assembly and sought for eternal life /A

Death and life **were made just the same for him, by the high gods."** /A

The scorpion-man raising his voice to be heard, said to Gilgamesh, /A

"**Do not trouble yourself with it**, Gilgamesh, the way is impossible /A

Not one man has successfully crossed the mountainous expanse /A

After just twelve leagues of traversing this tract **you will be lost** /A

The dark is far too pervasive, there is no light with which to see   /A

You must know the dawn **is a formidable distance, the way hard**   /A

You must know the dusk **is a formidable distance, the way uneven,**   /A

Yet to the dusk **is a distance once measured by kings of your kind**   /A

Who sent forth **a survey team to record the distance, here to there**   /A

But as for you, how is it that you **would be able to survive the way?**   /A

Are you going there **by yourself, and making this journey alone?**   /A

For while the expedition went forth and covered the entire space,   /-[39]

They were incapable of making it back again, and never returned   /-

And so they discovered the answer but none ever came to know it   /-

So don't be so hasty thinking that you can get there easily yourself   /-

It is worse when you return, when you deem the worst behind you."   /-

Gilgamesh raising his voice to be heard, said to the scorpion-man,   /(A)

"My friend was a mule pursued, a feral ass, a leopard of the plains   /(A)

Together we climbed the foothills up into the precipitous country,   /(A)

We took hold of the Bull of Heaven and brought about its demise   /(A)

We destroyed Humbaba, the terrible guardian of the Pine Forest   /(A)

Together we killed lions that lived in the dark mountain passes."   /(A)

The scorpion-man raising his voice to be heard, said to Gilgamesh,   /(A)

"If you truly destroyed Humbaba, the guardian of the Pine Forest,   /(A)

Who has killed predators living in the dark mountain passes,   /(A)

Who took hold of the Bull of Heaven, bringing about its demise,   /(A)

Then tell me why you look so gaunt, why is your face so troubled   /(A)

Why is your spirit so bleak, why do you resemble a vagabond   /(A)

And harbor a kind of misery which imbues your deepest frame?   /(A)

You wear an expression resembling that of a world-worn traveler   /(A)

You have a face lashed by the bitter wind and burned by the sun,   /(A)

And wearing only a lion-skin do you traverse the wilderness."   /(A)

Gilgamesh raising his voice to be heard, said to the scorpion-man,   /(A)

"Why would I not look gaunt, why would my face not be troubled,   /(A)

Why would my spirit not be bleak, why would I not be worn out   /(A)

Why would I not harbor a misery that imbues my deepest frame?   /(A)

Why would I not have the expression of a world-worn traveler   /(A)

Why would my face not be stricken by the cold wind and the sun,   /(A)

Why would I not traverse the wilderness, wearing only a lion-skin   /(A)

When my friend, who I loved so, and met every peril with me,   /(A)

When Enkidu, who I loved so, and who met every peril at my side,   /(A)

The friend who I loved so, he has been reduced to dust and clay   /(A)

Enkidu the one I loved so, he has been reduced to dust and clay   /(A)

And is my life not the same, that I must lie never again to rise?"   /(A)

Gilgamesh raising his voice to be heard, said to the scorpion-man,   /(A)

"So then, guardian, do you know the way to reach Utnapishtim?   /(A)

Tell me which way to go; as they stand, what direction from here   /(A)

Tell me if it might be done, whether I must traverse the open sea   /(A)

Because if it is not possible, I will go back into the wilderness   /(A)

Beset with a sorrow which strikes me to my very core do I come   /A

It is from the heat and the cold wind that my face is so stricken   /A

And I am exhausted by the journey I have made to arrive here   /A

So now you must tell me what I ask of you, and must not refuse."   /A

He, raising his voice to be heard, said to **the god-man** Gilgamesh, /A

"Then proceed on your way, Gilgamesh, **if you're intent on going** /A

Know that the peaks of Mashu **rise above a very long passageway** /A

The mountains **are wide, stretching the entire way the sun takes** /A

Go with caution, **make your way to the end, and there is a barrier*** /A

So too the front gate into the land of **Utnapishtim, the faraway."** /A

So Gilgamesh heard the words of the scorpion-man, **the sentinel**, /A

He went on the way of Shamash, **not a safe one but a straight one** /A

After he had gone one league, there was deep dark and little light /A

He could not make out that which was before him or behind him, /A

After he had traveled two leagues **he went on his way rapidly** /A

With deep dark and little light, he could not see before or behind /(A)[40]

After he had traveled three leagues he went on his way rapidly /(A)

With deep dark and little light, he could not see before or behind /(A)

After he had traveled four leagues **he went on his way rapidly** /A

With deep dark and little light, he could not see before or behind /A

After he had traveled five leagues **he went on his way rapidly** /A

With deep dark and little light, he could not see before or behind /A

After he had traveled six leagues **he went on his way rapidly** /A

With deep dark and little light, he could not see before or behind /A

After he had traveled seven leagues **he went on his way rapidly** /A

With deep dark and little light, he could not see before or behind /A

After he had traveled eight leagues **he went on his way rapidly** /A

---

* Gilgamesh is here travelling through the tunnel which is the passage of the sun.

With deep dark and little light, he could not see before or behind /A

After he went nine leagues his face **was hit by** the North Wind /A

With deep dark and little light, he could not see before or behind /A

After he had traveled ten leagues, the end was getting very close /A

After he had traveled eleven leagues, there remained but one left /A

After he traveled one league he emerged on the far side of the sun /A

He was forced to shield his eyes from the bright glow around him /A

In view were all manner of sharp and thorny bushes about him /A

Each of them was flowering with the richest of gems and crystals /A

There the *carnelian* was prolific, with dangling fruit so appealing /A

The *lapis lazuli* sprouted leaves, with ruby fruit so pleasing to see /A

Every sort of tree was present, formed of the most exquisite stones /-[41]

There were cedar and myrtle, cypress **and oak, even** pine **groves** /A

What is so rare and valued elsewhere was common enough there /-

So even the weeds and bramble glittered with semi-precious stone /A

There was wealth and plenty **everywhere he looked, riches for ages** /A

There it spread out like **an ocean of** turquoise, **as broad as** the sea /A

Impossible to fathom, it extended for leagues in every direction /-

Gilgamesh made his way through, **but there was also a girl there** /A

She looked up **to keep her eye on him, and see what he was up to** /A

(It was the beer-maid Siduri, who has her abode by the seashore)

TABLET X

It was the beer-maid Siduri, who has her abode by the seashore,   /A

There she lives and **brews the beer which is served to the gods**   /A

And she is provided with golden vats set up upon brazen stands   /A

She was draped in a full dress, **her face hidden beneath a veil**   /A

Gilgamesh was treading aimlessly about the place, **looking it over**   /A

Dressed in only a lion-skin, **he had the appearance of a vagabond**   /A

But his body glowed with the character of the divine element   /A

He harbored a kind of misery which imbued his deepest frame   /A

The expression he took was like that of a world-worn traveler   /A

The beer-maid observed him from her place a distance from him   /A

She wondered within herself, speaking to herself, and considered,   /A

"Maybe he's a killer, and looking around in search of his prey,   /A

But what might his intentions be, making his way to my gate?"   /A

So as the beer-maid kept an eye upon him, she latched the door   /A

She locked the bar with a bolt and secured it firmly with a catch   /A

Then when Gilgamesh became aware **of this, he raised his chin,**   /A

Gilgamesh spoke that his voice might be heard, to the beer-maid,   /A

"Beer-maid, why is it when you saw me you latched your door?   /A

You locked the bar with a bolt and secured it firmly with a catch   /A

Realize that I can break down the door, violate your precious lock   /A

Look at me again, and gaze upon this sore-stricken face of mine   /A

Know then that I have become a companion of the wilderness."   /A

The beer-maid, raising her voice to be heard, spoke to Gilgamesh,   /A

98

Tablet X

It is because you dress like a vagabond that my door is barred,   /A

And you could be a killer, so I bolted and secured it with a catch   /A

It will remain so until you tell me who you are and where you go."   /A

Gilgamesh spoke that his voice might be heard, to the beer-maid,   /A

"My friend was a mule pursued, a feral ass, a leopard of the plains /A

Together we climbed the foothills up into the precipitous country,   /A

We took hold of the Bull of Heaven and brought about its demise   /A

We destroyed Humbaba, the terrible guardian of the Pine Forest   /A

Together we killed lions that lived in the dark mountain passes."   /A

The beer-maid raising her voice to be heard, spoke to Gilgamesh,   /A

"If you really are Gilgamesh as you claim, who slew the sentinel,   /A

Who destroyed Humbaba, terrible guardian of the Pine Forest,   /A

Who has killed predators living in the dark mountain passes,   /A

Who took hold of the Bull of Heaven, bringing about its demise,   /A

Then tell me why you look so gaunt, why is your face so troubled,   /A

Why is your spirit so bleak, why do you resemble a vagabond,   /A

And harbor a kind of misery which imbues your deepest frame?   /A

You wear an expression resembling that of a world-worn traveler   /A

You have a face lashed by the bitter wind and burned by the sun   /A

And wearing only a lion-skin do you traverse the wilderness."   /A

Gilgamesh then spoke to her, saying to the beer-maid Siduri,   /A

"Why would I not look gaunt, why would my face not be troubled,   /A

Why would my spirit not be bleak, why would I not be worn out,   /A

Why would I not harbor a misery that imbues my deepest frame?   /A

Why would I not have the expression of a world-worn traveler,   /A

Why would my face not be stricken by the cold wind and the sun,   /A

Why would I not traverse the wilderness, wearing only a lion-skin,   /A

When my friend, who I loved so, and met every peril with me,   /A

When Enkidu, who I loved so, and who met every peril at my side,   /A

The destiny which awaits all mortals did likewise conquer him?   /A

Upon him I cried for six days and as many intervening nights   /A

But I would not let them bury him 'til a worm fell from his nose   /A

I was so scared and fearful **to think that he had been overcome**   /A

So fearful am I of impending death that I wander the wilderness   /A

But the words which were spoken by my friend do beset me so,   /A

For which I traverse the countryside over such great distances   /A

But the words which were spoken by my friend do beset me so,   /A

For which I traverse the countryside over such great distances   /A

How could I then remain quiet, how then not speak a word of it   /A

The friend who I loved so, he has been reduced to dust and clay   /A

Enkidu the one I loved so, he has been reduced to dust and clay   /A

And is my life not the same, that I must lie never again to rise?"   /A

The beer-maid raising her voice to be heard, spoke to Gilgamesh,   /B

"Gilgamesh, what is your destination as you search aimlessly?   /B

No matter how far you roam, you'll not find your eternal youth,   /B

For when the gods made man they set death as his ultimate fate   /B

Made him to live as a mortal and held eternity in their keeping   /B

Thereby, Gilgamesh, enjoy a full stomach, live in mirth every day   /B

Plan delights for yourself, both night and day be joyfully engaged   /B

Tablet X

Dress yourself in fine clothing, bathe yourself and wash yourself   /B

Find your good in the child you walk with, the wife at your bosom   /B

These alone are the things **which a mortal man** might strive for[*]   /B

Be not inclined to seek more than what the living **might enjoy."**   /B

Gilgamesh then spoke to her, saying to the beer-maid Siduri,   /B

"Is this your final word, beer-maid, **the only comfort you provide**?   /B

When I have no relief from the loss of my dearest friend, Enkidu   /B

From where you live on the sea you can see everything **beyond**   /B

So then, beer-maid, do you know the way to reach Utnapishtim?   /A

Tell me which way to go; as they stand, what direction from here   /A

Tell me if it might be done, whether I must traverse the open sea   /A

Because if it is not possible, I will go back into the wilderness."   /A

The beer-maid raising her voice to be heard, spoke to Gilgamesh,   /A

"There has never been a craft to ferry someone across the water   /A

And no one since the beginning of time has ever traversed the sea   /A

The warrior Shamash alone crosses that sea, but no one else has   /A

The way across is itself next to impossible, and the path is hard   /A

And there in the midst are the Waters of Doom to inhibit you   /A

So by what means would you be able to get across, Gilgamesh?   /A

When you have come to the Waters of Doom, tell me, what then?   /A

But, Gilgamesh, there is Urshanabi the boatman of Utnapishtim   /A

You will know him by his lodestones, which are objects of rock   /A

You will find him in the woods, chipping bark from a baby pine   /A

Go see him and whether he will take you, otherwise turn back."   /A

---

[*] These lines are comparable with Ecclesiastes 9:7-9

As soon as Gilgamesh heard this, he grabbed the axe beside him   /A

He unsheathed his sword, marched up and caused them to flee[*]   /A

Fast as a dart he quickly leapt among them and took them on   /A

The sound reverberated through the very depths of the forest   /A

Urshanabi heard this, took up his sword and axe and went forth   /A

And as he was coming up, Gilgamesh struck him upon his head   /A

He held his arms fast and **bound them to the front of** his chest   /A

The great lodestones **were then held in the bottom of** the boat   /A

They **would help in the** Waters of Doom, **to traverse** broad seas   /A

In the water **he thought to himself they might be** a hindrance,   /A

So he smashed and threw them, with a great rage, out of the craft   /A, B

After he had finished disposing of them he drove the ship ashore   /-

Then pulled the boat upon the bank, **and stood over Urshanabi**   /A

Gilgamesh raised his voice to be heard, to Urshanabi the boatman, /A

"As you might by no means obstruct me, I will gain free passage   /A

Tell me your **name, and how you are associated with Utnapishtim."** /A, B

Urshanabi the boatman looked at Gilgamesh and spoke to him,   /B

"I am Urshanabi, and am the man of Utnapishtim, the faraway."   /B

Gilgamesh raised his voice to be heard, to Urshanabi the boatman, /(A)

"Look at me again, and gaze upon this sore-stricken face of mine /(A)

Know then that I have become a companion of the wilderness /(A)

You must have heard of me, I am the King of Uruk, Gilgamesh, /(A)

And I have journeyed to the east through the mountain range."   /B

Urshanabi raised his voice to be heard, speaking to Gilgamesh,   /A

---

[*] There is no indication as to the identity of these guardian adversaries he confronts.

Tablet X

"Tell me why you look so gaunt, why is your face so troubled,   /A

Why is your spirit so bleak, why do you resemble a vagabond,   /A

And harbor a kind of misery which imbues your deepest frame?   /A

You wear an expression resembling that of a world-worn traveler   /A

You have a face lashed by the bitter wind and burned by the sun   /A

And wearing only a lion-skin do you traverse the wilderness."   /A

Gilgamesh raised his voice to be heard, to Urshanabi the boatman, /A

"Why would I not look gaunt, why would my face not be troubled,   /A

Why would my spirit not be bleak, why would I not be worn out,   /A

Why would I not harbor a misery that imbues my deepest frame?   /A

Why would I not have the expression of a world-worn traveler,   /A

Why would my face not be stricken by the cold wind and the sun,   /A

Why would I not traverse the wilderness, wearing only a lion-skin? /A

My friend was a mule pursued, a feral ass, a leopard of the plains   /A

My friend Enkidu was a mule pursued, a feral ass, a wild leopard   /A

Together we climbed the foothills up into the precipitous country,   /A

We took hold of the Bull of Heaven and brought about its demise   /A

We destroyed Humbaba, the terrible guardian of the Pine Forest   /A

Together we killed lions that lived in the dark mountain passes   /A

Enkidu, my friend, who I loved so, and met every peril with me,   /A

Enkidu, the one I loved so, and who met every peril at my side,   /A

The destiny which awaits all mortals did likewise conquer him   /A

Upon him I cried for six days and as many intervening nights   /A

But I would not let them bury him 'til a worm fell from his nose   /A

I was so scared and fearful **to think that he had been overcome**   /A

So fearful am I of impending death that I wander the wilderness /A

But the words which were spoken by my friend do beset me so, /A

For which I traverse the countryside over such great distances /A

But the words which were spoken by my friend do beset me so, /A

For which I traverse the countryside over such great distances /A

How could I then remain quiet, how then not speak a word of it /A

The friend who I loved so, he has been reduced to dust and clay /A

Enkidu the one I loved so, he has been reduced to dust and clay /A

And is my life not the same, that I must lie never again to rise?" /A

Gilgamesh raised his voice to be heard, to Urshanabi the boatman, /A

"So, Urshanabi, do you know the way to reach Utnapishtim? /A

Tell me which way to go; as they stand, what direction from here /A

Tell me if it might be done, whether I must traverse the open sea /A

Because if it is not possible, I will go back into the wilderness." /A

Urshanabi raised his voice to be heard, speaking to Gilgamesh, /B

"I can take you to Utnapishtim, the faraway, if we go in my craft /B

I will take you to the place upon earth where the flood arose." /B

Then they sat down together to work out a problem they faced, /B

Because Urshanabi had something to relate to the other man, /B

Urshanabi raised his voice to be heard, speaking to Gilgamesh, /A

"You, by the work of your own hands, have impeded **your way** /A

You, Gilgamesh, have broken the lodestones, **tossed them aside** /A

The lodestones have been broken to bits, their **cords ripped out** /A

The lodestones allow me to cross, so the Waters of Doom lie inert /A

But you in anger smashed every one of them, casting them over   /A

And it was these lodestones which guaranteed my safe passage   /A

So grab your axe, Gilgamesh, the one which hangs beside you   /A

Go into the forest and cut down 300 poles, each 30 yards long   /A

Even them out, put ends on them, and then bring them to me."   /A

As soon as Gilgamesh heard this, he grabbed the axe beside him,   /A

He unsheathed his sword, and made his way into the woodland   /A

There he cut down 300 poles, each one being 30 yards in length   /A

Then he evened them and carved a knob on every one of them,   /A

Then he brought them back to Urshanabi, waiting at the boat,   /A

Gilgamesh went with Urshanabi and they boarded their craft,   /A

They cast off in the cargo boat, and went sailing on their way   /A

Then after a journey taken from the new moon to the full moon,[*]   /A

After the span of just three days **they had come to the boundary**   /A

Urshanabi had taken them to the edge of the Waters of Doom   /A

Urshanabi raised his voice to be heard, speaking to Gilgamesh,   /A

"Take care, Gilgamesh, and now you will use each pole in turn,[†]   /A

By no means let the Waters of Doom touch you, grasp the knob!   /A

Then, Gilgamesh, take up the second, third, and fourth pole   /A

Then, Gilgamesh, take up the fifth, the sixth, and seventh pole   /A

Then, Gilgamesh, take up the eighth, the ninth, and tenth pole   /A

Then, Gilgamesh, take up the eleventh pole and the twelfth pole."   /A

After they had gone 720 yards, Gilgamesh had utilized every pole   /A

---

[*] A month and a half

[†] Seemingly he is unable to raise the pole to reuse it, and thus must use one pole per push.

At that he then released his belt, **letting drop his sash and robe** /A

Gilgamesh took off everything covering him, **tied the cloth tightly,** /A

And lifted up in his arms the crosspiece, making himself a mast /A

Standing at a distance with arms akimbo, Utnapishtim watched /A

He wondered within himself, speaking to himself, and considered, /A

"Why are the lodestones gone, and why the improper tackle used? /A

It must not be my man arriving. There **is another** upon his right /A

Although I can see with my eyes it is not clearly apparent to me, /A

Although I can see **there must be something strange is going on** /A

Although I can see **there is clearly something unusual afoot here."** /A [42]

As the boat came ever nearer to shore, Utnapishtim said to himself, /-

"Why are the lodestones gone, and why the improper tackle used? /(A)

It must not be my man arriving. **There is another upon his right** /A

Although I can see with my eyes it is not clearly apparent to me, /(A)

Although I can see there must be something strange is going on /-

Although I can see there is clearly something unusual afoot here." /-

The boatman **is surely Urshanabi, and him I clearly recognize** /A

But the other man who **accompanies him I haven't seen before,** /A

The one who **is standing up in the boat, taking the role of a mast** /A

Utnapishtim, the far away, watched the boat come in to shore, /-

As Gilgamesh directed it into the harbor, **steering them to land** /A

Urshanabi and Gilgamesh then brought the cargo boat to shore /(A)

When they pulled it up onto the land the man approached them /-

Gilgamesh spoke that his voice might be heard, to Utnapishtim, /A

"Are you Utnapishtim, **the man who survived the Great Flood,** /A

Who after the Great Flood **received immortality from the gods?"** /A

Utnapishtim raised his voice to be heard, speaking to Gilgamesh, /-

"I am Utnapishtim, the faraway, and Urshanabi is my boatman /-

But you are not known to me, and this is not a place much visited." /-

Gilgamesh spoke that his voice might be heard, to Utnapishtim, /(A)

"Look at me again, and gaze upon this sore-stricken face of mine /(A)

Know then that I have become a companion of the wilderness /(A)

You must have heard of me, I am the King of Uruk, Gilgamesh, /(A)

My friend was a mule pursued, a feral ass, a leopard of the plains /(A)

Together we climbed the foothills up into the precipitous country, /(A)

We took hold of the Bull of Heaven and brought about its demise /(A)

We destroyed Humbaba, the terrible guardian of the Pine Forest /(A)

Together we killed lions that lived in the dark mountain passes." /(A)

Utnapishtim raised his voice to be heard, speaking to Gilgamesh, /A

"Tell me why you look so gaunt, why is your face so troubled /A

Why is your spirit so bleak, why do you resemble a vagabond /A

And harbor a kind of misery which imbues your deepest frame? /A

You wear an expression resembling that of a world-worn traveler /A

You have a face lashed by the bitter wind and burned by the sun /A

And wearing only a lion-skin do you traverse the wilderness." /A

Gilgamesh raised his voice to be heard, speaking to Utnapishtim, /A

"Why would I not look gaunt, why would my face not be troubled, /A

Why would my spirit not be bleak, why would I not be worn out, /A

Why would I not harbor a misery that imbues my deepest frame? /A

Why would I not have the expression of a world-worn traveler, /A

Why would my face not be stricken by the cold wind and the sun,   /A

Why would I not traverse the wilderness, wearing only a lion-skin? /A

When my friend, who I loved so, and met every peril with me,   /A

When Enkidu, who I loved so, and who met every peril at my side, /A

The destiny which awaits all mortals did likewise conquer him   /A

Upon him I cried for six days and as many intervening nights   /A

But I would not let them bury him 'til a worm fell from his nose   /A

I was so scared and fearful **to think that he had been overcome**   /A

So fearful am I of impending death that I wander the wilderness   /A

But the words which were spoken by my friend do beset me so,   /A

For which I traverse the countryside over such great distances   /A

But the words which were spoken by my friend do beset me so,   /A

For which I traverse the countryside over such great distances,   /A

How could I then remain quiet, how then not speak a word of it   /A

The friend who I loved so, he has been reduced to dust and clay   /A

Enkidu the one I loved so, he has been reduced to dust and clay   /A

And is my life not the same, that I must lie never again to rise?"   /A

Gilgamesh raised his voice to be heard, speaking to Utnapishtim,   /A

"So I decided that I would seek out Utnapishtim, the faraway,   /A

He whom the people spoke of, so I sought through every land   /A

I made my way into and through a great many hard countries   /A

And have traversed my way over and across every body of water   /A

Never was I able to get enough sleep, I was so sorely beset inside   /A

And from this deficiency of sleep did I become even more restless   /A

But then I must ask myself what good it does me to suffer so?   /A

The beer-maid was not welcoming, with my garments like rags   /A

I have hunted the bear, hyena, lion, leopards, tigers, and deer   /A

Mountain goats, buffalo, and other wild animals of the country   /A

And I consumed their meat, and I lay out their hides to lie upon   /A

So let her secure her door against misery with tar and pitch!   /A

It is all because of me that games are ruined, **festivity languishes**   /A

And my former cheerful, carefree spirit has given way to despair."   /A

Utnapishtim raised his voice to be heard, speaking to Gilgamesh,   /A

"Then for what reason, Gilgamesh, do you protract your suffering? /A

When the gods created you, you received divine and mortal being   /A

When the gods caused you to be just as your father and mother,   /A

The fate of death will arrive at every mortal's door sooner or later,   /A

Whether he be Gilgamesh or some miserable or foolish wretch   /A

But for you there is set a throne in **the midst of** the assembly hall   /A

While the foolish wretch collects the waste instead of fine butter   /A

He receives the refuse and the leavings as his equal **to banquets**   /A

He wears only a loincloth, and goes about like **the savage man,**   /A

Whose belt is a simple piece of rope rather than a splendid sash   /A

And what comes from his lips is **senseless, so none seek his advice**   /A

He has no words of worth **to pass along to those seeking wisdom."**   /A

Think twice about this, Gilgamesh; **be aware of the difference,**   /A[43]

For who is the master of all the different **classes of mankind?**   /A

Would you compare yourself with Sin and Bel, **and Shamash,**   /A

When Sin journeys ceaselessly, and the gods are not fatigued   /A

They are always awake, **never given to rest, going on their ways,**   /A

The gods are always awake and never rest, going on their ways,   /A

From the very start of your life you had the support of the gods   /A

Rather think of what is proper, in a manner suitable for a man   /A

Do not forget your obligations, and to make your suitable gifts   /A

Otherwise, if Gilgamesh will not, then none will honor the gods   /A

And the holy shrines of the goddesses will be left in desolation   /A

They will no more remember the gods, and no longer feed them   /A

No matter how far you roam, you'll not find your eternal youth   /(B)

For when the gods made man they set death as his ultimate fate   /A

They gave him the gift of life but held eternity in their keeping   /A, B

But there is no possibility that they will ever bestow it unto man   /A

And this is what was designed to be the way for all of humankind   /A

Thus too it befell Enkidu, when the gods had determined his fate   /A

So then I ask what reason have you endured this foolish exercise?   /A

Why have you made yourself fatigued from a deficiency of sleep?   /A

For you have only caused your body to be imbued with misery   /A

By this you have only encouraged your fateful end to stalk nearer   /A

The fame of man is made to fall like a reed cut in the marshland   /A

Whether it be a noble youth or a chaste girl, Death claims them   /A

There are none who see its coming, nor can look upon its face   /A

There are none who can make out the voice of Death when near   /A

The fury of Death is a mower of men, cutting him to the ground   /A

And we might construct mansions or build a haven for ourselves,   /A

But it is all split apart by the brothers who did gain the legacy   /A

At times arise anguish through the land, when the river swells   /A

Tablet X

It exceeds its banks and brings about widespread flooding /A

The dragonflies flit upon the river, gazing upon the Sun's halo /A

But it follows after this, in the twinkle of an eye, that all is gone /A

Those who merely sleep and those who are dead then are alike /A

You cannot hope to portray the features of Death with your pen /A

Thus the uncivilized man is made no different than the student /A

Upon the day they blessed me, the great Anunnaki gods met /A

The one among them who decrees fate, Mammitum, was there /A

They decided among themselves to set forth both life and death, /A

They did not set a limit for the days of death, but did for life." /A

(Gilgamesh then raised his voice to Utnapishtim, the faraway)

TABLET XI

Gilgamesh then raised his voice to Utnapishtim, the faraway,	/A
"The way I see you, Utnapishtim, you do not look exceptional	/A
You appear no different from me, and I'm quite sure you are	/A
And I had been motivated to pit myself against you in a fight,	/A
But now that I am standing before you my limbs hang listlessly	/A
So tell me how you came to be within the company of the gods	/A
And end up in the god's gathering and receive eternal youth?"	/A
Utnapishtim raised his voice to be heard, speaking to Gilgamesh,	/A
"Allow me to disclose a closely guarded secret to you, Gilgamesh,	/A
And I will reveal to you something of the mysteries of the gods	/A
The city of Shuruppak you must surely have heard of before	/A
There upon the Euphrates, that was an ancient citadel indeed,	/A
Even when its divinities deemed the high gods generate a flood	/A
There were father Anu, the warrior Ellil, the supreme authority,	/A
Nimrod the chamberlain, Ennugi who controlled the canal locks,	/A
And keen-eyed Ea took an oath too, swearing himself to secrecy,	/A
Thus he conveyed their discussions to the wall of a reed hovel,	/A
'Hear me reed hovel, reed hovel, hear brick wall, brick wall,	/A
Reeds, hear every utterance! Bricks, attend to my every word!	/A
Take apart your house and with the timbers construct a boat	/A
Put aside your property and instead seek out living beings	/A
Disregard your possessions and instead save living things,	/A
And load aboard the germ of every living being in that boat	/A

Tablet XI

The boat you construct must be sized with proper proportion /A

Both the length of it and the width of it should be equivalent /A

And put a roof upon it, like that which covers the deep Apsu.' /A

I apprehended what was happening, replying to my lord Ea, /A

'I've heard everything that you conveyed as you have, my lord, /A

And so I will act accordingly, doing precisely as you told me /A

But what will I say to satisfy the men and elders of the city?' /A

Ea raised his voice to be heard, speaking to me, his servant, /A

'Tell them you are convinced Ellil has abandoned you, saying, /A

No longer will I be able to remain within your city walls /A

Never again will I be able to set my feet upon Ellil's fine land /A

But rather down into the Apsu must I travel, to be with Ea /A

If I do this then he will cause it to rain plentifully for you, /A

He will send down a wealth of fowl and a treasure of fish /A

He will shower a downpour of prosperity, like a cornucopia /A

In the morning he'll make it spread over you like thick syrup /A

In the evening you will drown in an abundance of heaps.' /A

"Thus when the first signs of dawn appeared the next day, /A

The people of the land assembled at the gate of Atrahasis:[*] /A

The carpenter with his axe, the reed worker with his stone, /A

And the ship-builder bearing his weighty shipwright's axe /A

The youth **and children came to me with stocks of bitumen,** /A

The elder gentlemen brought with them bundles of oakum, /A

---

[*] Another name for Utnapishtim

113

And the poor folks fetched **everything else** that was required /A

On the fifth day I was then able to lay out the frame's form /A

It spanned over the area of an acre, with walls ten poles high /A

Then I designed its form, drew out the plan for her decks /A

The craft was given six decks, and divided into seven levels /A

In her midst, however, I caused it to be divided into nine /A

And had bilge drains opened along the ship's mid-section, /A

Set to having oars made, and ordered in what was required /A

There was three loads of bitumen which I had put in the kiln /A

And three loads of pitch was poured down to seal the insides /A

Then three loads of oil brought by the men who carry baskets /A

Not counting the further load of oil that was lost to the dust /A

Further, the helmsman stowed an additional two loads of oil /A

Then for the workers' provision I had a large ox slaughtered /A

And to feed them every day I slaughtered a fine fat sheep /A

Giving them ale and beer as if there were no tomorrow /A

Pouring out oil and wine to the workers as if it were water /A

Every day was like the feast at the New Year's Day festival /A

When the sun appeared on the final day I gave them balm /A

By the time the sun **had set that day**, the boat was finished /A

But **the launching of the craft** proved of the greatest trouble, /A

And rollers had to be utilized and set from stem to stern /A

Until two-thirds of its hull **had descended into the water** /A

I loaded it with everything collected there, every bit of silver, /A

And every bit of gold, and the germ of every living being, /A

Tablet XI

I brought on board every one of my family and relations, /A
The cattle that inhabited the countryside I had brought in, /A
And every kind of wild animal which inhabits the wild lands, /A
Also every manner of skilled craftsmen did I bring within, /A
Shamash determined the time that the flood would come, /A
'In the morning I'll make it spread over you like thick syrup /A
In the evening I will drown you in an abundance of heaps /A
It will rain plentifully, enter the boat and seal the entrance.' /A

"The time had come, in the morning to spread like thick syrup, /A
In the evening an abundance of heaps, of rains in plenitude /A
And I looked aloft so I could see how the storm appeared /A
And I had never seen before such an ominous maelstrom, /A
I entered the boat and then closed up the door with pitch /A
To do so I gave charge of this buoyant bastion and load, /A
Gave control of her to the boat's helmsman, Puzur-Amurru /A
And with the first rays of the dawn came a blackened cloud, /A
Rising from the very foot of the horizon, as Adad boomed, /A
With Shullat and Hanish walking ahead like chamberlains,[*] /A
Before his throne they marched, over mountain and meadow /A
And Errakal ripped out every one of the pins from their bars, /A
Nimrod came on hard causing the breach of every blockade /A
The great ones, the Anunnaki, were required to bear torches /A
And these illuminated the country with their radiant light /A

---

[*] These two gods are associated with stars found around *Centaurus*. (see White 2008: 206)

This tranquility emerged prior to the coming of the storm god /A

When all that had been light was swallowed into the darkness /A

He reared up and went about to trample **the terror-stricken** /A

Upon the first day the tempest rose, blowing in an awful fury, /A

It **unleashed** the dreaded Flood-weapon, and like a war raged /A

The explosive annihilation-weapon descended over the people /A

And after this a person could no longer make out his fellow /A

They lost sight of one another in the sheets of cascading rain /A

Even the gods were alarmed by the full force of their flood /A

They retreated to the safety of the highest heaven of Anu /A

Where they cowered like dogs, kneeling by an outlying wall /A

Belet-ili was screaming in a frenzy, like a woman in travail, /A

The pleasing-voiced Mistress of the Gods was shrieking, /A

'Has this era truly come to its final finish, returning to clay, /A

From my willingness to utter evil at the gathering of gods? /A

Rather I should have waged war so as to eradicate my kith /A

It was I who gave them birth, they are truly my own children, /A

But now they are awash within waves like so many poor fry!' /A

The great ones, the Anunnaki, were likewise in a dire humor, /A

There they stayed, brought to their knees, and crying tears, /A

Their lips did not utter and were foaming over with spittle /A

Wind raged six days and seven nights, the tempest prevailed /A

Then upon the seventh day; the winds, water, and violence; /A

A turbulence no less severe than from a woman giving birth, /A

Then had their brutality wane, and the waters grew tranquil /A

Tablet XI

The terror-gust died down, and the raging flood relented	/A
And when I looked to see the state of things, all was quiet	/A
But then every man and woman had been reduced to clay	/A
The flood-waters around were entirely level just like a roof	/A
And when I opened the window, light beamed onto my face	/A
And I knelt down and sat, then cried with tears cascading,	/A
As I looked out for the hills and for the banks of the ocean	/A
And ridges of land were breaking the surface of the water	/A
The boat had settled itself upon the mountain of Nimush	/A
Nimush took hold of the craft and would not let it wander	/A
For the first and second days, the mountain of Nimush	/A
Kept the boat still, and did not allow her to move an inch	/A
For the third and fourth days, the mountain of Nimush	/A
Kept the boat still, and did not allow her to move an inch	/A
And for the fifth and sixth days, the mountain of Nimush	/A
Kept the boat still, and did not allow her to move an inch	/A
Upon the seventh day I reached out and set free a dove	/A
The dove flew out and came back, finding no place to perch	/A
Then I stretched forth my hand and released a swallow	/A
The swallow flew here and there, then came back home	/A
With no promising place it might alight upon, it veered	/A
After this I extended out my hand and released a raven	/A
The raven flew and seeing that the waters were receding	/A
It settled to eat, preen, and fluff itself, and did not return	/A
Then I released everything in all directions, and sacrificed	/A

The Gilgamesh Cycle

Setting down the incense offering upon the mountain peak	/A
Having my jars set out in seven columns and seven rows	/A
Into them I had poured the oils of reed, pine, and myrtle	/A
The gods smelled the rising smoke, a pleasing fragrance,	/A
And they gathered over the offering like a swarm of flies	/A
Immediately when the Mistress of the Gods had appeared,	/A
She held aloft the weighty flies given by Anu to win her favor,	/A
'Know then, great gods, that I will never forget these things,	/A
And may my *lapis lazuli* necklace become a reminder to me,	/A
So that I will recall this and never forget what happened here	/A
Other gods may be welcome to partake of the incense-offering	/A
But not Ellil, he should not be welcome at the incense-offering[*]	/A
He did not bother to seek counsel before unleashing the flood	/A
And so he thereby condemned my poor children to oblivion!'	/A
"Then when Ellil came he spied the boat, and was left enraged,	/A
He was fuming over with hostility at the gods of the Igigi,[†]	/A
'Did some form of life survive? None should have escaped!'	/A
Nimrod raised his voice to be heard, saying to the warrior Ellil,	/A
'There is none other who would but Ea, for he is omniscient!'	/A
Ea raised his voice to be heard, speaking to the warrior Ellil,	/A
'Ellil, foremost warrior, you are the wise counselor of the gods,	/A
Why did you not seek counseling before unleashing the flood?	/A

---

[*] This might thus explain a ritualistic detail, of Ellil not receiving the incense offering.

[†] Gods of the sky

The one who does wrong is blameworthy for his own wrongs   /A

And the one who commits crime culpable for his own crimes   /A

Refrain or you will snap the cord, back off or you will **break it**   /A

Rather than releasing a flood, the lion will reduce his numbers   /A

Rather than releasing a flood, the wolf will reduce his flocks,   /A

Rather than releasing a flood, famine will come, fields wither,   /A

Rather than releasing a flood, let war and plague decimate him,   /A

But I am not guilty of having divulged the high gods' secrets   /A

A dream came upon Atrahasis, thereby he came to know them,   /A

So then determine yourself what ought to be done with him.'   /A

Then Ellil approached the craft, and took my hand, lifting me,   /A

Then too he brought up my wife and she knelt down beside me   /A

Standing between us, with his hands to our heads, he blessed us,   /A

'Before this day Utnapishtim was as mortal as any other man   /A

But from this day forward he and his wife will be like the gods   /A

And Utnapishtim will now live at the distant source of rivers.'   /A

So they set me down to live at the distant source of the rivers   /A

"But who would be able to bring the gods together for your sake,   /A

That you might come to have the eternal youth you seek after?   /A

In the first place, you must lie awake six days and seven nights."[*]   /A

Then immediately when he sat with his head upon his knees,   /A

Then sleep came over him and settled upon him just like a fog   /A

Utnapishtim raised his voice to be heard, speaking to his wife,   /A

---

[*] Sleep being the brother of Death. (see *Iliad* xvi, 785)

"Here, take a look at this young man who seeks eternal youth!   /A

The sleep came over him and settled upon him just like a fog!"   /A

Then his wife raised her voice to Utnapishtim, the faraway,   /A

"Jostle him that he be awakened, so he may go away in peace   /A

Back to his own land via the massive gate, his former way out."   /A

Utnapishtim raised his voice to be heard, speaking to his wife,   /A

"Mankind cannot be trusted, so too he will try to deceive you;   /A

First, bake for him a daily allotment of bread, placed at his head   /A

Then mark the wall, one tick for each day he remains asleep."   /A

She baked a daily allotment of bread for him, placed at his head   /A

And marked the wall, one tick for each day he remained asleep   /A

The amount from the first day went dry, the second worsened,   /A

The amount from the third day was damp, the fourth moldy,   /A

The amount from the fifth day was turning, the sixth still ok,   /A

With the seventh baked, then he jostled him and awoke him,   /A

Gilgamesh then raised his voice to Utnapishtim, the faraway,   /A

"Why, just as soon as I fell asleep you jostled me, and awoke me!"   /A

Utnapishtim raised his voice to be heard, speaking to Gilgamesh,   /A

"But wait, Gilgamesh, count the number of daily allotments here   /A

Thereby you might know the number of days you were asleep   /A

The amount from the first day went dry, the second worsened,   /A

The amount from the third day was damp, the fourth moldy,   /A

The amount from the fifth day was turning, the sixth still ok,   /A

With the seventh baked, just then I jostled you and you awoke   /A

Gilgamesh then raised his voice to Utnapishtim, the faraway,   /A

"But then what am I to do now, Utnapishtim, and where travel?   /A

The thieves have made impassible **the way I might have taken**   /A

And no matter where I flee, Death is inevitably awaiting me   /A

Even in the security of my own bedroom I am not safe from him."   /A

Utnapishtim then raised his voice, to his boatman Urshanabi,   /A

"Urshanabi, you will find yourself cast from aside this wharf,   /A

You will be forsaken by the ferryboat, no longer her companion,   /A

For the man you brought here; his matted hair clinging to him,   /A

With the animal skins that have left hidden his fine physique,   /A

Remove him, Urshanabi, take him to the bathhouse at once!   /A

So that he might clean his dirty hair, as much as is possible,   /A

Discarding his animal skins, to be drawn away by sea currents,   /A

And leave him to soak in the bath until he is completely clean   /A

Then give him a fresh headband, dress him in a majestic robe   /A

To wear until he reaches his own city, and the end of his travels   /A

So the finery will never fade, but be kept as it was the first day."   /A

Urshanabi then led him out and took him to the bathhouse   /A

So that he cleaned his dirty hair, as much as he was able to,   /A

Discarded his animal skins, drawn away by the sea currents,   /A

And was left to soak in the bath until he was completely clean   /A

Then put on a fresh headband and dressed in a majestic robe   /A

To wear until he reached his own city, at the end of his travels   /A

The finery would never fade, but be kept as it was the first day   /A

Gilgamesh went with Urshanabi and they boarded their craft,   /A

They cast off in the cargo boat, and went sailing on their way /A

Then his wife raised her voice to Utnapishtim, the faraway, /A

"Gilgamesh, when he came to us, he was tired from his seeking /A

So what then might there be for him to take home with him?" /A

Then Gilgamesh, from the distance where he was, lifted a pole /A

And he guided the boat again to the shore, coming alongside /A

Utnapishtim raising his voice to be heard, said to Gilgamesh, /A

"Gilgamesh, when you came you were tired from your seeking /A

So then what might there be for you to take home with you? /A

I will reveal to you, Gilgamesh, a very closely guarded secret /A

Let me disclose something which the gods have left concealed /A

There exists a plant which has roots resembling the box-thorn /A

The thorns of this plant are much like a rose, and will prick you /A

But if you can attain this plant, you will find **eternal youth.**" /A

And right after Gilgamesh had heard this, he opened the pipe /A

Then used a cord to tie a weighty stone to each one of his feet /A

So that they pulled him all the way down into the deep Apsu /A

There he spied the plant and took it up, and it pricked him /A

After that he cut the weighty stones away from off of his feet /A

And then he was spit out by the sea, tumbling upon its shores /A

Then Gilgamesh raised his voice to Urshanabi, the boatman, /A

"Urshanabi, this plant will now provide alleviation to a curse /A

With it a mortal man might gain for himself the breath of life /A

I must take it back with me to the city of Uruk, the Sheep Pen, /A

There I will give it to a man old in years to eat, to test the plant /A

Tablet XI

Let it be called: 'the old man who becomes a young man again'   /A

And I then will eat of it, becoming the youth I had once been."   /A

After going a distance of 20 leagues they ate what food they had   /A

After going for 30 leagues they stopped to camp for the night   /A

Then Gilgamesh spotted a pool of water that was refreshing   /A

And he lowered himself into the water so as to bathe himself   /A

But a serpent scented the sweet smell that the plant exuded   /A

So that it approached with stealth and stole the plant away   /A

As it was leaving with it, the serpent shed its skin of scales   /A

Gilgamesh crouched low and tears rained down his cheeks   /A

Then Gilgamesh raised his voice to Urshanabi, the boatman,   /A

"What good, Urshanabi, has the toil of my arms been to me?   /A

And what good has the expenditure of my blood been to me?   /A

For I have gained nothing, only benefitting the dirt's predator   /A

But now the water currents have brought us twenty leagues   /A

Yet when I lifted the pipe's lid I abandoned my tackle there,   /A

And what could I utilize as a landmark to find my way back?   /A

So I will forsake my quest, to abandon the boat upon the bank."   /A

After going a distance of 20 leagues they ate what food they had   /A

After going for 30 leagues they stopped to camp for the night   /A

They journeyed all the way, before reaching Uruk, the Sheep Pen   /A

Then Gilgamesh raised his voice to Urshanabi, the boatman,   /A

"Climb upon the wall circling Uruk, Urshanabi, and traverse it   /A

Take a look for yourself at the foundation stones and the bricks   /A

You will see for yourself that these are the best of bricks, baked!   /A

The Seven Sages being the only ones who could have set its base   /A

Within is one square mile of housing, one square mile of orchard,   /A

Another square mile of clay pits, not to mention the courtyard   /A

This being the square in the temple of Ishtar, Queen of Heaven   /A

The temple grounds and the three square miles make up Uruk."   /A

(It was when the days were young, the time of the very first days)

TABLET XII

It was when the days were young, the time of the very first days /S

It was when nights were young, the time of the very first nights /S

It was when the years were young, the time of the very first years /S

It was the foremost of time, when all things had to be generated /S

It was the foremost of time, when all things had to be succored /S

And for the first time, in the earthly shrines, was bread baked, /S

And for the first time, in the earthly homes, were ovens fired, /S

At that time the heaven distanced itself, ascending from earth, /S

At that time the earth distanced itself, descending from heaven, /S

At that time when mankind was so named, as it has continued, /S

When Anu went up to heaven, when Ellil made his way to earth, /S

And Ereshkigal, Queen of Earth, gained her abysmal kingdom /S

Then he made his way by sailing, the Master went out sailing /S

Ea, the god of wisdom, went by sail, bound for the Underworld /S

Being beset by the small and large hailstones which pelted him, /S

And the small ones were fist-sized, the large ones shook trees /S

Charging like a gang of turtles, filling up the hull of Ea's craft /S

The waves of the sea ate his bow like the teeth of ravening wolves /S

The waves of the sea pounced against his stern like violent lions /S

It was then that a tree, the one and only tree, the lofty *huluppu*** /S

Was set into dirt upon the wind-swept shore of the Euphrates /S

The tree received all its nutrients from the rich Euphrates water /S

---

* Perhaps the date palm, a tree associated with Inanna (Ishtar)

125

But the sweeping South Wind blew, tearing both root and stem,   /S

Until the swelling currents of the Euphrates bore it silently away   /S

And then a noblewoman passed,* who feared the word of Anu   /S

A noblewoman sauntered by, one who feared the word of Ellil   /S

And she drew the tree from out of the river's currents, and spoke,   /S

"I will take this tree with me to the city of Uruk,   /S

Providing it sanctuary in my own sacred garden."   /S

She did not plant it with her hands, but set it in dirt with her feet   /S

She did not water it with her hands, but watered it with her feet   /S

"How long must I wait before I have a stunning throne to sit on?   /S

How long must I wait before I have a gleaming bed to rest upon?"   /S

The years went by, first five years passed, then ten years passed,   /S

And the tree attained a wide girth, yet its bark did not split apart   /S

But an insufferable serpent nested among the roots of that tree   /S

The Anzu-bird placed its younglings in the branches of the tree   /S

The night maiden Lilith built her home in the depths of its stem   /S

So that young lady who was given to laughter was driven to tears   /S

How Ishtar cried at this, still they would not abandon her tree   /S

Morning birds heralded the coming of the day's dawn as it broke   /S

Shamash rose from his stately slumber; she spoke to her brother,   /S

"Shamash, in early days when fates were planned,   /S

And plenty was spread thick throughout the land,   /S

When Anu received the sky and Ellil the earth   /S

---

* This being the goddess Ishtar

126

And the great Abyss was made Ereshkigal's abode /S

Then my father Ea, god of wisdom, set sail alone /S

Bound for the Underworld, but they set upon him /S

Then that tree, the one and only tree, the *huluppu* /S

Stood on the wind-swept shore of the Euphrates, /S

Where South Wind mightily tore root and stem, /S

Until Euphrates' currents bore it silently away /S

Thus it was that I pulled it from churning waters, /S

Providing it sanctuary in my own sacred garden, /S

Caring for it, anticipating my throne and bed /S

But then a serpent, who could not be tempted, /S

Nested itself among the roots of my poor tree; /S

Its branches came to be used as the dwelling /S

Of the infamous Anzu-bird and its younglings; /S

When the night maiden Lilith happened upon it /S

She built her home within the depths of its stem /S

And I cried, oh how I cried, but they did not leave!" /S

The brave warrior Shamash didn't lift a finger for his sister Ishtar /S

Morning birds heralded the next day's dawn as it was breaking /S

And Ishtar raised her voice, speaking to her brother Gilgamesh, /S

"Gilgamesh, in early days when fates were planned, /S

And plenty was spread thick throughout the land, /S

When Anu received the sky and Ellil the earth /S

And the great Abyss was made Ereshkigal's abode /S

Then my father Ea, god of wisdom, set sail alone /S

The Gilgamesh Cycle

Bound for the Underworld, but they set upon him /S

Then that tree, the one and only tree, the *huluppu* /S

Stood on the wind-swept shore of the Euphrates, /S

Where South Wind mightily tore root and stem, /S

Until Euphrates' currents bore it silently away /S

Thus it was that I pulled it from churning waters, /S

Providing it sanctuary in my own sacred garden, /S

Caring for it, anticipating my throne and bed /S

But then a serpent, who could not be tempted, /S

Nested itself among the roots of my poor tree; /S

Its branches came to be used as the dwelling /S

Of the infamous Anzu-bird and its younglings; /S

When the night maiden Lilith happened upon it /S

She built her home within the depths of its stem /S

And I cried, oh how I cried, but they did not leave!" /S

The brave warrior Gilgamesh did act in favor of his sister, Ishtar /S

So Gilgamesh then strapped his fifty *minas* of armor about him /S

This fifty *mina* load seemed as weightless to him as fifty feathers /S

He raised his brazen blade, his travel axe, set it upon his shoulder /S

A bronze axe weighing a full seven *talents* and seven more *minas* /S

He set forth and came through the gate of Ishtar's sacred garden /S

Gilgamesh hit the insufferable serpent, who was not easily swayed /S

The Anzu-bird and its younglings flew to the mountainous tracts /S

Lilith demolished her home and fled into the vacant wilderness /S

So Gilgamesh tore out the roots which secured the *huluppu* tree /S

Tablet XII

The young men of the city, who were with him, sawed off its limbs   /S

Wood from the trunk was made into a throne for his holy sister   /S

Planks from the trunk were formed into a bed frame for Ishtar   /S

Then she took up its roots and made a ball fit for her brother   /S

From a tree limb she made a mallet for Uruk's hero, Gilgamesh[*]   /S

Then he took up his ball to go play with it in the public square   /S

And he took up his mallet to go play with it in the public square   /S

And with the city's young men, he played sport with the ball   /S

Gilgamesh sat on the shoulders of a team of these widows' sons   /S

They cried out, "O how my neck strains! O how my hips hurt!"   /S

If he had a mother she came with bread,   /S

If he had a sister she brought him water,   /S

Then at dusk, Gilgamesh made a mark where his ball landed   /S

And then took it up and carried it with him back to his house   /S

But at dawn, having found this mark, he climbed on shoulders,   /S

And because the widows cried out, and the young girls did weep,   /S

Then did the ball fall, descending down into the Underworld   /A

So too did the mallet fall, descending down into the Underworld   /A

Gilgamesh raised his voice to be heard, speaking to Enkidu,[†]   /A

"If only I had left the ball within the house of the carpenter!   /A

---

[*] These are the *pukku* and *mekku*, which seem to be a specialized sort of mallet and ball used for a game.

[†] This is thus not chronologically placed, but is from a Sumerian episode appended here to the Akkadian version as Tablet XII. The Sumerian episodes concerning Gilgamesh were not strictly unified as they are within the later Gilgamesh Cycles (see Introduction).

Carpenter's wife, who is like a mother to me, had I only left it,   /A

Carpenter's daughter, who is like a sister to me, had I only left it   /A

But today the ball fell down, descending into the Underworld   /A

And the mallet made for me went down into the Underworld."   /A

Then Enkidu raised his voice to be heard, speaking to Gilgamesh,   /A

"For what reason do you weep, my brother, being so saddened?   /A

I should be able to raise the ball again from the Underworld   /A

I should be able to raise the mallet again from the Underworld."   /A

Then Gilgamesh raised his voice to be heard, speaking to Enkidu,   /A

"If you descend into the Underworld, then pay heed to my advice   /A

Don't dress in clean clothes or they'll think you're not one of them   /A

Likewise, do not put upon yourself any perfume from the oil jar,   /A

They would flock around you if they caught a whiff of that scent   /A

Likewise, don't fling your throwing-stick into the Underworld,   /A

For any knocked by the throwing-stick will gather around you   /A

Do not lift up a mace in your hand, for spirits will flit about you   /A

Go unshod, for otherwise you'd make a racket under the Earth   /A

Do not kiss your most beloved wife, nor smack your despised wife   /A

Do not kiss your most beloved son, nor smack your despised son   /A

For there will be an uproar in the Underworld directed at you   /A

Ninazu's mother,* never failing to sleep, who lounges all the time,   /A

She allows no fabric to obscure her splendidly washed shoulders   /A

Her bosom assertive, unlike an oil jar carried in a leather satchel."   /A

But when Enkidu made his journey down into the Underworld,   /A

---

* Ereshkigal, Queen of the Underworld

Tablet XII

He was heedless of the advice his lord Gilgamesh had given him,[*] /A

He dressed in clean clothes, so they knew he was not one of them /A

Likewise, he put upon himself perfume taken from the oil jar, /A

And they flocked around him when they caught a whiff of it /A

Likewise, he flung his throwing-stick far into the Underworld, /A

So those knocked by the throwing-stick gathered around him /A

He lifted a mace in his hand, and the spirits flew about him /A

He shod his feet, thus making a great racket beneath the Earth /A

He kissed his most beloved wife, and smacked his despised wife /A

He kissed his most beloved son, and smacked his despised son /A

And there was an uproar in the Underworld directed at him /A

Ninazu's mother never failing to sleep, who lounges all the time, /A

She allows no fabric to obscure her splendidly washed shoulders /A

Her bosom assertive, unlike an oil jar carried in a leather satchel /A

When Enkidu attempted to make his way out of the Underworld /A

He was not held back by either Namtar or Asakku, but by Earth /A

The one hunched, Ukur the relentless, did not hold him back, /A

It was Earth that held him back, the Underworld that kept him /A

And the son of Ninsun left and cried for his manservant Enkidu, /A

Going away by himself to Ekur, to the temple of Ellil, saying, /A

"Master Ellil, today my ball descended into the Underworld /A

And the mallet made for me went down into the Underworld /A

When Enkidu descended to recover them, Earth held him back /A

---

[*] In the Sumerian tales Enkidu is portrayed as a servant of Gilgamesh

131

He was not held back by either Namtar or Asakku, but by Earth   /A

The one hunched, Ukur the relentless, did not hold him back,   /A

It was Earth that held him back, the Underworld that kept him   /A

He did not drop in a battle among men, but the Earth took him!"   /A

But master Ellil did not reply to him, so he went to Sin's temple   /A

"Master Sin, today my ball descended down into the Underworld   /A

And the mallet made for me went down into the Underworld   /A

When Enkidu descended to recover them, Earth held him back   /A

He was not held back by either Namtar or Asakku, but by Earth   /A

The one hunched, Ukur the relentless, did not hold him back,   /A

It was Earth that held him back, the Underworld that kept him   /A

He did not drop in a battle among men, but the Earth took him!"   /A

But master Sin did not reply to him, so he went to Ea's temple   /A

"Master Ea, today my ball descended down into the Underworld   /A

And the mallet made for me went down into the Underworld   /A

When Enkidu descended to recover them, Earth held him back   /A

He was not held back by either Namtar or Asakku, but by Earth   /A

The one hunched, Ukur the relentless, did not hold him back,   /A

It was Earth that held him back, the Underworld that kept him   /A

He did not drop in a battle among men, but the Earth took him!"   /A

Master Ea did reply to him, saying to the fighting man Ukur,*   /A

"Ukur, belligerent young man, **I have a task for you to perform**   /A

Go and clear a passage through the Earth at this very moment,   /A

To release the spirit of Enkidu from the Earth like a wind blast   /A

---

* Nergal, king of the Underworld

132

Tablet XII

So he might again be in the company of his brother Gilgamesh." /A

Ukur, the belligerent young man, **did what he had been ordered** /A

And he cleared a passage through the Earth at that moment /A

So the spirit of Enkidu came from the Earth like a wind blast /A

And they embraced one another and were ripe with fondness /A

Then they conversed between themselves, discussing the matter, /A

"My friend, when you were in the Underworld, what was it like?" /A

(Enkidu raised his voice to be heard, speaking to Gilgamesh,)

"I must not reveal it to you, my friend, I cannot reveal it to you /A

If I revealed what that place is like, you would fall and weep." /A

(Gilgamesh raised his voice to be heard, speaking to Enkidu,)

"If you reveal what that place is like, then I will fall and weep." /A

(Enkidu raised his voice to be heard, speaking to Gilgamesh,)

"Your friend to whom you showed affection, filling you with joy, /A

He was being consumed by so many pests like a worn-out dress /A

Enkidu the one whom you showed affection, filling you with joy, /A

He is sitting by himself in a fissure which is filled with dry earth." /A

"What misery!" he cried as he was falling down to the ground, /A

"What misery!" Gilgamesh cried as he fell down to the ground, /A

(Gilgamesh raised his voice to be heard, speaking to Enkidu,)

"And there did you happen to notice the father with one son?" /A

(Enkidu raised his voice to be heard, speaking to Gilgamesh,)

"Yes, where a nail is affixed to the wall, he cries harshly over it." /A

"And there did you happen to notice the father with two sons?" /A

133

"Yes, he consumes baked bread, resting himself on two bricks."   /A

"And there did you happen to notice the father with three sons?"   /A

"Yes, he consumes water from a water-skin draped on a saddle."   /A

"And there did you happen to notice the father with four sons?"   /A

"Yes, like the driver of four mules, his heart was in good spirits."   /A

"And there did you happen to notice the father with five sons?"   /A

"Yes, like the best of scribes who possesses a very felicitous hand,   /A

He goes in and about the citadel without a second thought of it."   /A

"And there did you happen to notice the father with six sons?"   /A

"Yes, like the man with a plow, his heart was in good spirits."   /A

"And there did you happen to notice the father with seven sons?"   /A

"Yes, he sits in honor judging matters among the lesser gods."[*]   /A

"And there did you happen to notice the father with no sons?"   /A

"Yes, he consumes bread as hard as a brick baked in a kiln."   /A

"And there did you happen to notice the king's chief eunuch?"   /A

"Yes, he was leaning over in the corner like a forsaken banner,   /A

Or as if he were **a discarded *alala*-stick propped up at an angle."**   /A[44]

"And there did you notice the woman who did not give birth?"   /S

"Yes, she is discarded like a cracked pot, no man delights in her."   /S

"Did you see the young man who did not take his wife to bed?"   /S

"Yes, he must labor on weaving a rope, and his tears fall over it."   /S

"Did you see the wife who refused to go to bed with her spouse?"   /S

---

[*] These appear to be numerical parallels: the single nail for one son, the two bricks for two sons, the water-skin and saddle represent three sons, the four mules for four sons, the fingers of a hand for five sons, the six legs of draught ox and plowman for six sons, and perhaps seven divine judges for seven sons.

"Yes, she must labor on weaving a mat, and her tears fall over it."   /S

"Did you see there the one who swore an oath and then broke it?"   /S

"Yes, he cannot get to the necessary location in the Underworld,   /S

Where offerings of water are provided, and so he goes thirsty."   /S

"And there did you notice the man who suffered from leprosy?"   /S

"Yes, and his food and drink were not the same as the others,   /S

He consumes grass, digs for water, and dwells outside the wall."   /S

"Did you happen to see there the man afflicted with pellagra?"   /S

"Yes, he is always twitching like an ox, as the worms eat him."   /S

"And there did you happen to notice the man eaten by a lion?"   /S

"Yes, he is forever crying out in agony, 'O my hand, O my foot!'"   /S

"And did you happen to notice the man who fell from a roof?"   /S

"Yes, he is always twitching like an ox, as the worms eat him."   /S

"And did you happen to notice the man drowned in a torrent?"   /S

"Yes, he is always twitching like an ox, as the worms eat him."   /S

"And did you notice the man who did not respect his parents?"   /S

"Yes, he is only allowed a modicum of water, and is always dry."   /S

"And did you notice the man who was a curse to his parents?"   /S

"Yes, he was never to have a son, and his spirit wanders still."   /S

"And did you happen to notice one struck by a mooring pole?"   /A

"Yes, he cries to his mother and father, for his ribs are split,   /S

His torso **is gaping wide, so he has no way to eat** his daily food."   /S

"Did you happen to notice stillborn children, who knew not life?"   /S

"Yes, they ate honey and butter at tables of silver and gold."   /S

"And there did you happen to notice him who burned in fire?"   /S

"Yes, his spirit was gone, for he ascended as smoke into heaven." /A

"And did you happen to notice one who came to an early end?" /A

"Yes, he spends his day lying in his bed and sipping clear water." /A

"And did you happen to notice one who was slain in bloody war?" /A

"Yes, he is honored by his parents and his wife laments for him." /A

"And did you notice one whose corpse was left in the wilderness?" /A

"Yes, his spirit is not settled in the Underworld, it wanders still." /A

"And did you happen to notice one whose spirit is fed by none?" /A

"Yes, he feeds on what is left upon the eating tables by others, /A

Consuming crumbs of bread which lie discarded in the streets." /A

And he was afflicted by a sad heart, his mind was depressed, /S

So the king was bent upon the quest to seek out eternal youth, /S

And his thoughts turned to the master of the gods' mountain* /S

(Of him who gazed upon the Abyss, which underlies the world)

---

* That is, Humbaba.

Bibliography

Dalley, Stephanie, trans. <u>Myths from Mesopotamia</u>. 1989. New York: Oxford, 2000.

de Santillana, Giorgio & von Dechend, Hertha. <u>Hamlet's Mill: An Essay Investigating the Origins of Human Knowledge and its Transmission through Myth</u>. 1969. Boston: Godine, 1977.

George, Andrew, trans. <u>The Epic of Gilgamesh</u>. 1999. London: Penguin, 2003.

Kramer, Samuel & Wolkstein, Diane. <u>Inanna: Queen of Heaven and Earth</u>. New York: Harper & Row, 1983.

Sandars, N. K. <u>The Epic of Gilgamesh</u>. 1960. London: Penguin, 1972.

Stephany, Timothy J. <u>Blood & Incest: The Unholy Beginning of the Universe</u>. printed by Createspace, 2013.

Stephany, Timothy J. <u>Roar of the Tempests: A Dialogue</u>. printed by Createspace, 2012.

Stephany, Timothy J. <u>The Death of King David: A Dialogue</u>. printed by Createspace, 2012.

Stephany, Timothy J. <u>The Eden Enigma: A Dialogue</u>. printed by Createspace, 2012.

Stephany, Timothy J. <u>The Zodiac Mysteries</u>. printed by Createspace, 2012.

White, Gavin. <u>Babylonian Star-Lore</u>. London: Solaria, 2008.

Endnotes

[1] White (2008), p. 77.

[2] White (2008), pp. 79, 169.

[3] White (2008), p. 34.

[4] Staal (1988), p. 43 and Krupp (1991), p. 138.

[5] see de Santillana (1977), pp. 419-421.

[6] see Charlesworth (2009), Vol. 2, p. 502.

[7] White (2008), p. 204.

[8] Tablet 2 begins with the first column missing, or an absence of about 45 unrecoverable lines. Given the emphasis within the Akkadian version upon Uruk, and that Enkidu would have perceived it for the first time around this point, here some lines from Tablet 1 have been transposed to fill in the gap.

[9] These lines have been partly constructed from the Akkadian version and partly from the Babylonian; the latter gives the sequence of Shamhat removing her clothes whereby they both robe themselves. I have presumed that after having seen the city of Uruk that Enkidu proved reluctant to remain before Shamhat encouraged him to go to the temple and pray to Ninlil, but this still remains speculative.

[10] These seven lines bridge a gap of about 40 lines which must have related to Enkidu becoming aware of what went on in the city of Uruk which caused him to then go with Shamhat to seek out one of the servants of the feast at the homes of the 'father-in-law', which is a generic term for the fathers of the brides (daughters-in-law) claimed by Gilgamesh the king. Without any other source to utilize, however, only a vague link might be produced.

[11] This link of three lines covers an irretrievable gap of more than 12 lines, which sets the stage for Enkidu going to confront Gilgamesh at last.

[12] There follows about 35 missing lines which can be partly reclaimed from the Old Babylonian version.

[13] These three lines are an attempt to bridge the broken columns of Tablet 3 of the Old Babylonian version, although about 30 lines are missing in column 1, there remains only the content of this single line. The following two arise from column 2 which begins with 12 missing lines, 4 fragmented lines, and 10 more missing lines. Little of this is recoverable before it links up again with the Akkadian version.

[14] There now follows a gap of about 30 lines which can be mostly filled from the Old Babylonian version.

[15] Here a gap of about 35 lines can be mostly filled in from the Old Babylonian version.

[16] From this point forward the reconstruction of Tablet 3 is difficult given its fragmentary condition along with the differences between the Akkadian and Old Babylonian versions here utilized.

[17] There is a slight gap of about three lines which cannot be recovered.

[18] These five lines have been borrowed from an episode slightly earlier on the same tablet.

[19] These six lines come from the address made by the elders, but as this has already occurred they have been inserted here, constituting the only legible lines from column 6.

[20] About 20 lines describing the dream at this point remain absent.

[21] There is a very large gap of about 60 lines, being virtually impossible to bridge except that clearly the third dream is interpreted and then they proceed on and encounter a pride of lions, which is then followed by six reconstructed lines from fragments.

[22] The description of their arrival to the lair, until Humbaba speaks, is preceded by a gap of several lines.

[23] Beginning with this line is a link to overcome about 60 unrecoverable lines. Nothing can be construed concerning the contents of this significant gap.

[24] The next several lines fill a gap of indeterminate length.

[25] There are about 15 unrecoverable lines before the next line starts.

[26] There follows an unrecoverable gap of about 45 lines prior to the next line.

[27] There follows a gap of about 15 lines, perhaps recoverable from the Old Babylonian version.

[28] There are about 30 missing lines which can be partly recovered from the Old Babylonian version.

[29] About 20 lines missing here can be partly recovered from a Hittite text.

[30] There follows about 50 unrecoverable lines revealing the close of the dream and response by Gilgamesh.

[31] There is a gap of about 30 lines through which Gilgamesh finally admits that Enkidu has died, part of which is found in the 'Megiddo Tablet', although the reconstruction is tentative.

[32] There follows here about 12 missing lines.

[33] There follows over 100 missing and fragmented lines detailing Enkidu's funeral preparations, some of which can be filled in from about 75 line fragments, probably detailing unique customs and not especially essential to the story of Gilgamesh.

[34] Ten fragmentary lines are summed up with this line, which indicate various items placed in Enkidu's tomb, each given a weight in minas.

[35] This and the next eight lines are used to fill in the gap and accommodate more fragmentary lines.

[36] There follows another gap consisting of the sixth column, probably detailing the funeral's conclusion.

[37] Here is a gap of about 13 missing and fragmentary lines.

[38] There is a gap of about 15 lines following.

[39] This is a significant gap of about 40 lines which can be variously filled.

[40] These three lines cover a gap of about 8 lines.

[41] There are here about 25 unrecoverable lines and this single line attempts to bridge this gap. The next three lines fill in for some fragmentary lines descriptive of the vegetation made of various kinds of rare stone. Little attempt has been made to preserve the precise language.

[42] There follows about 30 missing lines, partly filled in here from previous dialogue.

[43] The next few missing and fragmentary lines are very difficult to interpret.

[44] There follows about 25 unrecoverable lines, with a few similar lines inserted from the Sumerian version.

www.ingramcontent.com/pod-product-compliance
Lightning Source LLC
Chambersburg PA
CBHW070657290526
45790CB00001B/353